The Dating Repair Kit

How to Have a Fabulous Love Life

Marni Kamins and Janice MacLeod

Conari Press

First published in 2007 by Conari Press,
an imprint of Red Wheel/Weiser, LLC
With offices at:
500 Third Street, Suite 230
San Francisco, CA 94107
www.redwheelweiser.com

ISBN-10: 1-57324-283-7
ISBN-13: 978-1-57324-283-7
Library of Congress Cataloging-in-Publication Data available upon request

Book and cover design by Jessica Dacher
Typeset in Matrix Script, Bembo, and Berthold Akzidenz Grotesk

Printed in China
MD
10 9 8 7 6 5 4 3 2 1

To our sisters
Julie, Carla, & Piper

Contents

Part 1
Getting Started

How to Use This Book

Sit down. Get comfortable. This book is for when you want concrete answers to why dating sucks and you're tired of reading about how he's just not that into you or following rules such as waiting for "the call" and then pretending you're too busy to answer it. The dating world has lost its common sense. It has slipped so far into the darkness of rules and fears that people no longer feel safe about getting out there and would rather just sit at home alone.

The last U.S. census reported well over eighty-two million single people, most of whom probably want the same thing and yet are confused and frustrated by the search for The One.

Right now, perhaps you don't want to have to figure it out in therapy, write about it, or even talk about it. You don't even have to know what it is. Perhaps you simply have this overwhelming feeling that you can't deal and you don't know what to do about it. Maybe you feel like you just need more, but you don't know what *it* is that you need *more* of. More happiness? More fun? More help? More inspiration? More love? Who knows? It doesn't matter right now, because right now you don't have to do a thing. This book is intended to make life easier for you. Breathe deep. Relax. You are exactly where you are supposed to be.

Nourishing & Maddening Interruptions

So you were reading along and felt compelled to come over here and read this little distracting box. We scatter these through the book on purpose. Sometimes you come over and it's just a dumb quote by someone who could obviously deal. People like Henry David Thoreau, who by the way, sold all his stuff and moved into the woods with an axe to write his books. Clearly, could not deal. He worked pretty hard to find his muse. Why is it we put people on such pedestals? We are all just trying to do the best we know how to do. So when you find yourself reading these distracting boxes, think of them as a break. A nice little hiatus from focusing on the book. They are perfect for the short-attention span. Read, ponder a moment, look at your fingernails and then move on.

We highly suggest reading this book in a comfy chair, in bed, or sprawled out on the floor. Read it with a tasty snack and yummy tea between trips to your favorite distracting stores, because that is mostly how we wrote it. Feel free to read it on company time. You could sneak it into your office at work to read with the door closed, pretending you are very busy and not to be disturbed because some of it was written like that, too. If your attention span feels short and you want to jump from topic to topic, feel free to skip around because we wrote it like that, too. We can relate. We have looked at the greener grass on the other side and stared it down. While we don't believe in any particular rules in dating, we do believe in common sense. What we want this book to give you is more confidence, more fulfillment, and more hope. We will ease your mind and walk you through the first steps so you can get out there without freaking out.

We believe that while taking the steps necessary to get yourself ready to start your great love life can take you to a certain point, unless you are willing to take our suggestions emotionally and spiritually into your heart, your results may not be authentic. This book includes thirty days of things to do to attract more love into your life. The activities and exercises herein are designed to help you grow and heal from the inside out. It is hardly effective to think you can change patterns by just changing your outsides. So don't just read this book, ponder it so the ideas really sink in. Some of the activities may take you longer than one day depending on your circumstances. Conversely, you may feel compelled to do a few days at one time. Or, your

> *And the time came when the risk [it took] to remain tight in the bud was more painful than the risk it took to blossom.*
> —*Anaïs Nin*

situation may require you to jump around from day to day. That's fine. It's also okay if you skip a day here and there, but please try not to let the entire process run longer than forty-five days. This is a thirty-day course you're taking, and you owe it to yourself to stick to it. If you don't like our way after giving it your best shot, you can always go back to the way you've always done it. Be open to trusting this process. It really does work.

If at any moment while you're reading this book or taking steps "out there" you feel like you just can't deal, come back to this page and read this:

You are an amazing, creative, fun and passionate person. You are unique and irreplaceable in this world. Trust yourself and your process. Everything is exactly as it is supposed to be in this moment. We promise.

And remember, this book is your friend.

Day 1: Contemplating a Fabulous Love Life

Not all treasure is silver and gold, mate.
—*Capt. Jack Sparrow, Pirates of the Caribbean*

Ah, the fabulous love life. The focus of movies, songs, poetry, and even the news. It's our greatest inspiration and desire and it dramatically promises to save us from this dreary life, but it is also over discussed, misunderstood, and a huge source of frustration. And it's often the source of many a "my life would be perfect if only" thoughts.

What Is a Fabulous Love Life?

We do need each other. We need love, and we need to share love in order to blossom. It is our human instinct to connect with each other and form lasting, loving relationships. Sometimes we blame our crappy emotions on the behavior of someone else or simply the lack of someone else. We get mad or feel bad when we have to express our needs and then become frustrated when they still aren't met. We expect others to do what we ask, thinking that if they would just do so, then we wouldn't have any problems. This attitude won't get us anywhere, or at least not very far. But if we first focus on loving ourselves, we *will* attract the love of others.

A Great Love Life Starts with a Love Affair with Ourselves

A love affair with ourselves is not reliant on a relationship with someone else. When we have a great love life on our own, we are ready and open to having a truly great love life with someone else. A great love life on our own means we know how to love ourselves first; we know how to take care of ourselves and feel good about ourselves from the inside out with or without someone else. Our love life with ourselves should be like a fully baked cake, and a mate should just be the frosting. Cake is always great on its own, but frosting makes it so much better.

> *Conventional knowledge is death to our souls . . . .*
> *Live where you fear to live, destroy your reputation, be notorious.*
> —*Rumi*

If we strive for a mate to make us complete, we are striving for the wrong thing. All the love we need is within us right now. Seriously. Think about it: when you feel love, it is coming from inside of you; another person is just the catalyst that brings it out. We have searched the world—the States,

Canada, Australia, grad schools, French classes, twelve-step meetings, pints of ice cream, churches, synagogues, and the Internet—looking for love, only to discover it was inside us all along. Once we found love's place inside, great people came along to share it. Finding the love within can be easier said than done. This book is going to help you find it.

A Great Love Life with Yourself

Having a great love life is about knowing how to take loving care of yourself and having rituals in your life that make you happy. It's about having friends that you weave into your life regularly and who know you well. It's about having a favorite TV show that you look forward to watching every week and maybe having someone come over every Thursday to watch it with you. It's about enjoying waking up in your own warm bed and stretching and looking forward to making tea. It's about relying on yourself rather than another person for excitement and happiness. It's about attaining lots of love even if you aren't making love to a lover. (Though that will come later. Whooee!) It's about recognizing and being grateful for the people in your life that treat you with kindness and give you joy.

> *If you don't risk anything, you risk even more.*
> —Erica Jong

Having a love affair with yourself is going to a birthday party without a date and having full, entertaining conversations with boys, girls, couples, parents, aunts, and uncles, and being glad you are who you are. It's about being proud of yourself for being the best version of *you* you can be. It's about being satisfied that you are doing the best you can with what you've got.

A Great Love Life with Someone Else

A great love life together is when you both decide to learn about life alongside each other. Time spent with your partner is worth it even though you may not melt every time you see them. This person can turn from 100 percent perfect to 80 percent compatible or even just 80 percent tolerable, but for some reason that's beyond you, it's A-OK. This is the one you want to learn and grow alongside of and make a commitment with to stick together.

> Indeed love heals, but being loved does not. Being loved merely holds the door open for healing, for happiness, for fulfillment, for getting our needs met. But to walk through that door, we must love.
> —Hugh and Gayle Prather

A great love life with someone else is not perfect. If it was, how would we grow at all? How would we experience passion—good and bad? A great love life involves equal measures of work and play, but sometimes relationships feel so *serious* and we spend so much time *working* them out that we lose sight of whether or not we are capable of *playing* together. Love is about knowing when to laugh and play and remembering that without the down, there would be no up.

How to Have a Great Love Life in Five Easy Steps

Here is a quick cheat sheet in case you're impatient and want a great love life right here, right now. Feel free to refer to it when you're in the thick of the book. We suggest reading this page over a few times a week as you read through this book and *do the exercises* just to help remind you of the great love life you're working to achieve.

1. **Remove baggage.** Get rid of anything that is keeping you tied to your past. Remove the emotional and physical obstacles that may be keeping you from moving forward. Stop reading old love letters. Put away photos that make you ache. Even avoid as best you can energy-stealing family members and friends who bring you down. If you feel drained when you are around certain people, make a new point of avoiding them. If you don't like your living situation, start taking steps to move. If you feel you need therapy, get it. Resolve the unresolved. Today is the day.

2. **Fantasize.** Set the scene for what your ideal life will look like. Ask Spirit* to bring more love into your life. By keeping the focus on what we want for ourselves, we have a much better chance of experiencing those joyful things. Ponder plenty and start making your fantasies at least 50 percent believable. Making them 50 percent believable will help you stretch your imagination and strive for the deeper dreams.

3. **Take baby steps.** Take a look at one of your fantasies and pick a few small things to do to get the ball rolling. Set an intention to take action by a certain deadline. There is no such thing as not having enough time. This is your chance to decide what you really want and go after it. If you are serious about a great love life, you'll be willing to do something about it. Take note of any fears that arise when you start to take action and then do it anyway.

* When we talk about Spirit, we are referring to whatever spiritual guides you may believe in. We're not here to push some sort of religious deity down your throat. We are not going to argue with you about what Spirit is. Feel free to substitute Spirit for God, Higher Power, Buddha, the ocean, the collective unconscious, the power of electricity, or whatever power beyond yourself that you want to tap into that will assist you in bringing you closer to your great love life.

4. **Confront your excuses.** Deal with harmless little excuses that lead us back to the unhappy yet comfortable place we were before we started on this journey. "Harmless" excuses include flaking out on going to see a band you really like because you tell yourself you're too tired, or seeing the fantasy version of yourself as thinner or more buff than your current self but eating donuts because they are good and you can always be healthy *later*. Again, this is your only life. Why not start becoming the person you want to be right now?

5. **Date smarter**. We tapped into the wisdom of those who have great love lives (and those who really don't) so we could avoid the excruciating experiences and head straight to the learning. We consulted them and compiled what we learned so you don't have to waste time. For example, we discovered that guys will tell you who they are in the first few dates; they're not as mysterious as we thought.

Part 2
Remove Baggage

Day 2: Make Room for Love to Come In

*If you want the whole thing, the gods will
give it to you. But you must be ready for it.*
—Joseph Campbell

Okay. We know what you're probably thinking. Why do we have to get rid
of stuff to let love in, right? Can't we just be told what to do? Learn when to
call, when not to call, what to wear, what to do, what to avoid, what the rules are
already! Why focus on our *inside* when he is *out there*?

Wanting vs. Being Ready

There is a huge difference between wanting something and being ready to have it. If we were having someone over for dinner, we wouldn't mess up the house and forget to plan what to eat. We'd clean up and prepare to receive our guests. If we didn't plan ahead and they showed up, they would probably sense that we didn't want them to come over in the first place. We want our life to be a healthy, welcoming space for that person to enter.

You may say that all you really want in your life is to finally meet The One, but wanting to meet The One and being ready to be with The One are two entirely different things. For some, it seems that this special person comes along at the precise time that they were ready to meet. For others, it seems that they met The One and chucked him because they had too much other stuff to deal with. If meeting someone and falling in love is your true intention, start clearing that space right now. Throughout this section we will help you begin to let go of any baggage you no longer want to carry.

> *I'm gonna break*
> *I'm gonna break my*
> *I'm gonna break my*
> *rusty cage and run*
> *—Johnny Cash*
> *(covering Soundgarden)*

We are going to master the art of releasing who we were to make room for who we are to become. Yay! Start fantasizing about life the way you've always wanted it. You can have whatever you let yourself be ready for. You don't always get what you want, or what you *think* you'll be ready for after you make more money or lose ten pounds, but you get what you *are* ready for.

Setting the Stage

Our friend Jen had a pink bedroom. It was cute, but it was the kind of room that would be perfect for a ten-year-old girl. She was thirty. We asked her what guys thought when they saw her room. She stood there stunned and said, "It's never been a problem. Never made it to that point. I never seem to like anyone enough to bring them home. I never find anyone sexy."

Jen never found anyone sexy because she didn't feel sexy herself. Jen decided right then and there to make a change. She fantasized about what having a guy in her room would look like. She saw creamy walls, not pink. She saw neutral shades for her sheets and pillows. She saw candles. Then she redecorated according to her fantasy. She also discovered that the act of shopping for supplies made her excited and revved up about the possibility of meeting someone she really liked enough to bring into her sexy, grownup bedroom. She even met someone in the sheet section at Bed, Bath & Beyond.

> *Our job in this world is not to shape ourselves into some ideal we imagine we ought to be, but to find out who we already are and become it.*
> —*Steven Pressfield, War of Art*

They didn't get married, but they dated awhile and she learned that she could be open to new possibilities. Even if it just means new bedding.

Dressing the Part

Don't wear ugly undies. Your sexuality is a part of you just like your sense of humor or intellect. Don't turn it off because there isn't a guy around to see it. Wear undies that make you feel sexy. Trim up or shave your legs if that's what makes you feel good. Smell nice. Do what needs to be done to keep you from feeling like an asexual frump.

After a breakup, Marni stopped trimming and leg shaving. She figured no one would see her so why bother. One day she looked down and realized it was starting to look like a stray cat down there. Something had to be done. Her actions were showing her that she wasn't ready to meet someone even when her head was telling her she was. She trimmed and started wearing underwear she felt hot in. Two days later she met someone great!

The Old Has to Die for the New to Be Born

We are transitioning from our current state of *wanting* to our new state of *having* great love in our lives. That's why most journeys to improve our lives start with loss. The plan is to release all that isn't working or loving in our lives, thereby growing healthier, stronger, and more capable of creating a space for love to come in. For example, when Janice was going through a breakup, she met Marni and started writing books. A week after Janice got laid off from her job, she and Marni got a book deal. When Janice's roommate situation got cramped, she found the apartment of her dreams. If you let go gracefully now, it will be easier and faster to receive the life you are meant to lead later.

> *In the long run, we shape our lives, and we shape ourselves. The process never ends until we die. And the choices we make are ultimately our own responsibility.*
> —Eleanor Roosevelt

Friends: Love 'Em or Leave 'Em

What is dear to us and worth keeping? To many, friends are the most important. If your family members feel like your friends, feel free to include them in this process. However, if they don't, there is no need to fill them in on your new intentions. Dreams are precious. Don't share them with people who won't support them.

Today is a good day to get rid of anyone that you describe as a friend but clearly isn't one. Stop calling them if you can. You want support and love. If it doesn't feel like love, it's probably not. Getting rid of friends that don't support you is

> *Life consists of what a person is thinking about all day.*
> —Ralph Waldo Emerson

showing yourself love. When good friends hold you accountable, it feels like it is coming from a place of caring. When bad friends give you advice, it feels like your mojo is being squashed. Being around bad friends somehow always makes you feel tired and worse than before. Best to save your energy for your great love life, yes?

Stuff: When in Doubt, Throw it Out

While we're getting rid of unsupportive friends, we're also going to do some physical cleaning out. Literally. Drawers, closets, boxes of letters, saved e-mails from past loves, even old lip gloss you don't use anymore. Start getting rid of stuff. Go through your closet and get rid of clothes you don't wear anymore. Don't save too much for sentimental reasons, because after a while it just becomes more stuff that will weigh you down. If there are things that you are unwilling to part with, put them to the side. Ask yourself why you are saving all these things. Why do you think you need them? To feel less alone? To remind yourself of what once was? Because you might need it someday? As if you won't ever be able to get anything again.

> *You can't always get what you want,*
> *but if you try sometime you might find,*
> *you get what you need.*
> *—The Rolling Stones*

It is difficult to let go of something when it is still there staring us in the face. Ask yourself what are you afraid to let go of and what you are ready to allow in to take its place.

Four Great Reasons to Remove Baggage

1. **To indulge in those old broken-down relationships for the final time.** There is something juicy about reading those love letters for the last time. Sometimes we just have to get it out of our system before we move on. We will feel so much lighter.

2. **To learn what we truly want.** Delving into the past and being reminded about what didn't work and what did can bring to light what we truly want.

3. **To retain energy.** Relics of the past hold energy. Every time we look at a photo that reminds us of a past pain, it sucks out a little of our energy. If we have a lot of those relics around, we

> *For the most part, people most often choose comfort—the familiar, the time-honored, the well-worn but well-known. After a lifetime of choosing between comfort and risk, we are left with the life we currently have.*
> *—John-Roger and Peter McWilliams, authors*

start to feel drained, which doesn't help us get excited about creating a wonderful future. Instead, it supports us in being stuck in the past.

4. **To show Spirit that we are serious about letting love into our lives.** Removing baggage is serious business. Destroying, ripping up, ripping out, wiping away, deleting, selling and throwing out stuff of the old tells the Universe we are ready for something new.

Day 2 Exercise A: Find a Baggage Buddy

Before we begin to get rid of baggage, we like to find a baggage buddy for support. Sometimes baggage gets heavy and we need a strong friend to help us see what to toss and what to keep. Make sure that you have good friends that you can call at any time during this process of creating a great love life. Call your best friend and tell her you are committed to meeting The One, that there will be no more dilly dallying and dating men that live in other cities or that won't commit to calling you girlfriend if that's important to you. It may seem silly to call and say this aloud, but do it anyway. The power of an intention stated aloud to a friend can work miracles. Your friend will encourage and support you and hold you accountable if you go against yourself.

When we have been doing the same thing for a long time, it feels comfortable for us, and in many cases it feels like the right thing. We almost adopt it as a personality trait. When we are committed to doing something different than we have always done, it will not feel normal or right and understandably we will want to twist back into our old position. Good friends will be allies in your quest and hold you to your word. Plus, if you want to have space for a loving relationship in your life, it is important to practice love. Just like when you're learning to ride a bike, you need training wheels. Loving relationships with good friends are like training wheels for a loving relationship with a mate. After all, the best romantic relationships are actually really deep friendships.

Day 2 Exercise B: Let Your Soul Mate Know You're Ready

We seriously considered not putting this in the book. It is almost scary how powerful this prayer can be. Don't use this unless you are serious about wanting to call in your soul mate. If you don't feel ready to meet The One yet, don't use it, but since you're here reading this book, there is at least a part of you that is open. When you are ready you will know. If you are ready, recite this prayer everyday throughout the rest of the 30 days. If you say this with all your heart every day, powerful things will happen.

We received this prayer from our friend Brandi who got it from her friend who got it from her friend, and so on. We love that it's been passed through the sisters.

I draw to me my right partner, the soul whose love serves my soul's highest potential
The soul whom my soul enhances to highest potential
I draw this partner to me freely and lovingly as I am drawn to this partner
I choose and am chosen out of pure love, pure respect, and pure liberty
I attract one who attracts me equally
I attract a partner who is as willing as I to work at having and sharing a healthy relationship
I seek and I am found
We are a match made in Heaven to better this earth

Days 3–8: Remove Physical Baggage

Your task is not to search for love but to find
a portal through which love can enter.
—Eckhart Tolle, The Power of Now

Over the next week, we'll be cleaning physical baggage out of our lives. You can clean a little at a time or clean a lot if you get in a groove. Janice only likes to clean ten things at a time. That may seem like a lot, but if her room is a mess, she'll fold a sweater. That's one thing. Then she'll make the bed. That's two things. She'll throw a shirt in the hamper. That's three things. She'll do this until she gets to ten. Often once she gets to ten, she gets in a groove and finishes the room, but she doesn't feel obligated to do anything beyond ten things. Before you begin any clearing-out task, tell yourself the following:

This act of removing baggage will be easy and full of grace. It is in service to building the great life of my dreams.

To remember this phrase, you can copy it onto a card. Decorate it if you want. Then put it somewhere you'll read it often, like beside your alarm clock, on the refrigerator, or in an area you feel is cluttered. Often when we tell ourselves it will be easy, it becomes easy. Go figure. Also when we keep telling ourselves it's for our great love life, we start to have a great love life.

Day 3 Exercise: Clean Up the Bedroom

The bedroom or sleeping area is a good place to start since we want this to be a comfortable, loving, and inviting space for ourselves and perhaps someone else. If your room is frilly and stuffed with relics of the past—photos of old lovers, parents, high school friends, and so on, you may want to throw some out or at least file them away. And if you keep some photos of close friends of the opposite sex on display to secretly make someone new jealous, or to make yourself seem desirable to others, it will not help to attract more goodness into your life. Remember, water seeks its own level. Be ready to receive what you are really attracting. If you play games, you will attract games. If you manipulate, you will attract manipulation. Besides, you're beyond all that. That old way wasn't working. You have signed up for something new. Put the photos away, trash the holey undies, and start living for what you want.

Day 4 Exercise: Clean Out Your Clothes Closets

Get rid of the clothes that don't match you anymore. That could include the fat-day pants, the skinny pants you still think you'll fit into one day, and the concert T-shirt that only reminds you of the annoying drive home with your boyfriend and not the concert at all. Keep only clothes that fit the person you are today. Feel free to donate these clothes to a local charity or Goodwill as a means not only of giving but also drawing more good into your life.

Day 5 Exercise: Rethink Your Living Space

Is your living space a place where you can comfortably invite a lover? Janice had a roommate who said to her the day she moved in, "I'm a very private person. I don't like having people over to my house." This made Janice uncomfortable when the opportunity arose to invite her date inside. She spent a lovely evening out with him, he walked her home, and when they arrived at her door, she had to say goodbye, even though she didn't want to. What annoyed her was not that she *had* to let him go; it was that she didn't have the option to let him in. She wanted the option.

It dawned on her that if she was truly serious about having a boyfriend, she had to change her living situation. She couldn't live in a place where boys weren't allowed. Even if she was saving money by having a roommate, she was delaying her great love life. Her commitment to what she really wanted surpassed her desire to save money by having a roommate who didn't like houseguests. She moved out so she could invite him in. Now they are together.

It's easy to put up with "in the meantime" environments. Furniture we'll put up with because it's a hand-me-down from our aunts. It's not our taste but it'll do. Piles of paper that have to be dealt with. Projects that are half done that we don't get around to finishing. These spaces feel temporary, empty, and lacking in love. We want to surround ourselves with furniture and knickknacks that make us smile. If we are always eyeing the couch and wishing it was more comfy, or staring at the stack of papers in the corner and feeling lazy, on some level we are being drained. Surround yourself with items that bring you joy, not things that make you long for "one day when . . ."

Feng Shui is the ancient Chinese art of arranging items in a space to create better energy flow. You know when you arrange furniture and, though it looks fine, it doesn't feel right? Well, when you continue to rearrange until it *does* feel right, you are practicing Feng Shui. The space that feels "right" has more energy flow. Cluttering up a space can plug up the energy flow, too. Pack up the so-so knickknacks and donate them. You'll feel a weight has been lifted, and you'll gain a tax deduction.

Day 6 Exercise: Clean Up the Bathroom

Wow, is it easy to create clutter here! All those products and magazines can add up. Because this is usually the last room you're in before you go out for the evening, you could be taking some cluttered energy with you. Throw out expired products, samples you don't use, and hotel shampoos. And what about those ratty towels? What will you offer an overnight guest? The bathroom is a judgment zone. A nasty bathroom is not only uninviting but it can also be a little scary. Clean, well-organized bathrooms feel calm and reflect that you choose to live your life the same way.

When Janice went over to Marcus's house, she noticed that the spare bathroom that she used was full of bathroom supplies. The drawers and closets were so full of rolls of toilet paper and paper towels that there wasn't even room to store an overnight toiletry bag. Did this guy have a thing for Costco? This was a small thing but it just made her feel unwelcome and that Marcus's life was too full to include her in it. Her hunch was right. Eventually Marcus told her he had no room for her in his life.

Day 7 Exercise: Log Your Finances for a Month

If we want to be with someone who is in control of their finances, then we should strive to be on top of our own. Cancel services that you don't use but that still incur monthly charges—the Web site you bought but never created for the next big online experience, the gym membership you used twice, the monthly online music store you haven't visited since the first month you signed up. Consolidate your credit cards to just a few that you can pay off quickly and cancel high-interest, electronic-store credit cards. Get your tax information up to date and create an organizing system to keep your papers in order so you're super ready to get next year's taxes done when January rolls around. Keep a log for a month to see where you spend your money. Write down everything you spend and everything you earn. This act creates an immediate sense of understanding about your money. Plus the act of writing it down gets tiresome—tiresome enough to make you want to avoid spending. Cha-ching!

Day 8 Exercise: Clear Your Schedule

Do you have time for a fabulous love life? Or are back-to-back appointments your priority right now? Constant activity can be a way to avoid uncomfortable feelings like loneliness. The sooner you make friends with these feelings, the sooner they will change into something you no longer fear, allowing you to slow down and enjoy some much-appreciated alone time. Some of us also have jam-packed schedules because we would rather protect ourselves from the risks involved with falling in love than actually experience it. We do all kinds of stuff to avoid being hurt, including being too busy to dive into pursuing the love we desire.

You want to create breathing room in your day to fantasize about the great life you are going to have. This requires creative thinking. Creative thinking requires time to percolate. Clearing out time in your schedule may result in some uncomfortable feelings at first. These feelings are coming up to be healed. Thank goodness! Better to start healing them now rather than when you're already deep into a relationship. These feelings are coming up to help you prep for your relationship. Honor them. Feel them. Go to therapy to help name them. Ponder them and even indulge in them. Give yourself time to wallow in delicious memory. Indulge, wail, and suffer dramatically. Then move on.

Removing Physical Baggage Checklist

☐ My bedroom is a reflection of myself. It makes me feel sexy and comfortable.

☐ My closets are well-organized and only hold clothes that match who I truly am today.

☐ My living space is a place where I can comfortably invite a lover.

☐ My bathroom is neat and tidy and reflects the way I choose to live my great love life.

☐ I am on top of my finances. I have simplified my payment systems and know where all my money is and where it is going. If I'm not yet on top of them, I have a plan of action that I can follow one step at a time.

☐ I have cleared up my schedule and have made room in my life for love and fun.

Feel free to add a few more items to your checklist if you're removed more baggage than what's listed above.

☐ _____

☐ _____

Days 9–13: Remove Emotional Baggage

*We must be willing to get rid of the life we've planned,
so as to have the life that is waiting for us.*
—Joseph Campbell

Most of us desperately want with all our hearts to find a soul mate, a lover, and a best friend all rolled up into one, but we have been too scared to get in the game. Are we too afraid to visit the dark corners of our mind and sweep them clean or uncover what we never knew was there? What do we think we'll find when we get there? Today is the day to begin removing any blocks. Begin now. Don't wait. Time passes anyway.

Day 9 Exercise: Give Up How You Thought It Should Be

Sometimes how we thought it should be is a mix of what our parents wanted for us (often a reflection of what they missed out on), what we thought life would look like, what we see on TV, and what Disney dishes out. Imagine for a minute that it's not up to us what we get. The only thing we can do is show Spirit we're ready to receive, and we're going to spend our time being more loving to ourselves, knowing and believing this will draw love toward us.

Sometimes we like to think having a mate will fix everything: "If only I could find an amazing hottie, everything would get better." Okay, it might—for a week or two—but when the cocaine high of love wears off

you're right back where you started: wishing for someone to make it better. A mate will not fix you. Only you can fix you. A mate *may* bring up issues in your life that you can recognize as parts of yourself that need to be healed, but a mate will not fix your issues.

Sometimes a fear of being alone causes us to enter relationships for the wrong reasons. We are afraid we won't find someone better. He looks good on paper so we think the strong feelings will come. He provides us the attention our parents didn't. Or worst of all, he likes me and I just like feeling liked. A person who is unhappy before entering a relationship will most likely be unhappy during a relationship. Best to work on letting go of these expectations and concentrate on being happy in your life now so you can be happy when you meet someone special.

Imagine for a minute that you may not always know what is best for you. What hurts you today may turn out to be the best thing for you tomorrow. In fact, today's challenge may have been carefully disguised training that enables you to successfully overcome something new tomorrow. You will be provided with everything you need. *And you won't be given more than you can handle.*

Write down how you thought your life would be. Then write a letter to yourself from a wiser, older version of you who has seen it all. Here's an example from Janice's experience:

I thought I would find someone to marry in school. But now I've been out of school for many years. Where is he already?

Dear Janice,

Thank GOD you didn't marry that schmuck you were dating in school. What a horror show THAT would have turned out to be. I know you're frustrated, but the person you are meant to be with WILL come along and everything will happen just as it has to happen at the time. Boy oh boy, I'd love to tell you how you meet your husband because DAMN it's a good story, but I don't want to ruin the surprise. Just know that everything that is supposed to happen, does. Hang tight; you are well taken care of and it will all work out. Love ya honey. Breathe deep and keep on trucking.

With love,
Your older, wiser, and wrinkly self

Day 10 Exercise: Give Up an Addiction

Okay, we realize this may take a whole lot longer than one day, but today is just the day you may want to begin thinking about it. Today may also be the day you get yourself to a twelve-step meeting, even if it's just to check it out and to score karmic brownie points (mmm . . . brownies) for how well you're doing our program. So search your soul, think of something you'd like to quit, and check out a solution. We have a list of some of the many different twelve-step programs and their Web sites. If twelve steps isn't your bag, explore some alternatives with a counselor.

How can you have a relationship with some *one* when your primary relationship is with some *thing*? Giving up an addiction may unleash feelings you want to avoid. Avoidance is probably what started the addiction in the first place. It may feel uncomfortable and painful, but it will be that much more rewarding when you transform your life and let the love in. Go ahead and feel what needs to be felt, then proceed like a star.

> *If it makes you happy, why the hell are you so sad?*
> —Sheryl Crow

Reaching out to people for help with an addiction is important. Support groups are free and nonjudgmental. You may find out you're not as crazy as you thought. People share what is happening in their lives, and when you hear what they have to say, you may discover some of your own stories. Whether you choose to share or choose to listen, these people understand because they have gone through it all themselves.

Below are a few popular support groups:

- Alcoholics Anonymous: *www.alcoholics-anonymous.org*
- Adult Children of Alcoholics: *www.adultchildren.org*
- Al Anon/Alateen (For families of Alcoholics): *www.al-anon.alateen.org*
- Co-Dependents Anonymous (take the quiz on page 192!): *www.coda.org*
- Debtors Anonymous: *www.debtorsanonymous.org*
- Narcotics Anonymous: *www.na.org*
- Overeaters Anonymous: *www.overeatersanonymous.org*
- Sex Addicts Anonymous: *www.sexaa.org*

These groups suggest checking out at least seven meetings before you decide if a program is or isn't for you.

Day 11 Exercise: Victim Shmictim

> *Forgiveness is the fragrance*
> *a violet sheds on the heel*
> *that has crushed it.*
> *—Mark Twain*

So you've been hurt in the past. You may hold on to this hurt because you feel no one understands your pain. Or maybe you feel comfortable sitting in your own crap just because it's warm. Who wants to get up and have to clean up their own mess? Maybe you feel the world owes you a better hand of cards. Or perhaps you think forgetting the pain shows the perpetrator they've won. Could it be the whole "woe is me" thing is something you've done for so long that you don't know how to stop acting like a victim?

Some people like to wallow in past pain as if they are worshipping at a Shrine of Past Hurts they have built in their minds and continue to add to as more pain arrives. Ask Spirit for the strength and willingness to let go. Letting go means forgiving any debts you think you are owed by another or the world. It means you no longer want to spend time wishing the past had been different. Remaining a victim takes up a lot of the energy you could be putting toward love. Acting like a victim isn't fun. Being in love with life is fun. Holding on to your past can cost you future love. Let go, then forgive yourself for holding on. You don't have to agree with what someone did to you, but you can decide to forgive what happened. Forgiveness opens up space for love to come in. That's a really good reason to practice it.

> *It is our choices . . . that*
> *show what we truly are,*
> *far more than our abilities.*
> *—J. K. Rowling*

You don't have to decide you like the person who did you harm or think their life is admirable. To forgive someone doesn't mean you trust them or want them back in your life. (It may even be smarter not to invite them back.) Forgiving them is not about them; it's about you. It means that you understand that all anyone does is the best they can do at the time, even if it seems to you that they could have done much (much) better. True forgiveness feels like your emotions are no longer charged when you think of them. They are neither negative nor positive. They are just neutral. This neutrality is the space that is left over after we have removed the negativity that was blocking it. This space can now be used to let love flow for someone new.

To remove any lingering negative feelings:

- First, set the intention that you want to forgive this person in order to remove negativity from your life. There is tremendous power in intention.

- Second, let yourself feel any emotions that may arise.

- Third, sit in silence after you experience any emotions. This "sit in" helps seal the work you've done. Can you be okay with what has come up for you—positive or negative? This is a good time to check to see if your emotions are neutral. If they aren't, repeat this process until they are.

Janice Forgives Her Ex-Boyfriend

I never go to confession anymore. Yet one idle Saturday I found myself walking into a church while confession was in session. My original intention was to light a candle, say a prayer, and leave, but I found myself drawn to the confessional. I went in, sat with the priest, and told him I truly didn't consider the things I'd done to be sinful. He then asked me, "Then how can I help you feel peace?" I sat stunned and immediately felt words falling out of my mouth with no forethought. "I want to forgive my ex-boyfriend."

Then the tears came. The priest sat with me until my tears shifted from a river of choking snot to a whimpery stream of salt. Then he said, "I think you just have." Immediately I felt lighter. I felt that in this moment, I could move on and stop living my life according to how we had turned out. That night I had a dream. I sat with my ex-boyfriend and thanked him for what I had learned by knowing him. Then I released him from any karmic ties we might have had. I awoke and knew that by ending one chapter, I had allowed a new chapter to begin.

Day 12 Exercise: Give Up Unavailable Men

We don't *mean* to fall for all these unavailable men but dammit, doesn't it just keep happening? We keep getting tied up with people who are unwilling or unable to love us the way we want to be loved. It's torture to love and not be loved back. We hang on to hope in relationships, but it costs us emotion and energy that could be better spent creating something healthier for ourselves.

Enough with chasing unavailable people to try to get them to be available. "Unavailable" means married men, men with girlfriends (even if they say they are about to break up), men with boyfriends, men who *tell you* they can't commit, men who keep dumping you, men who cheat on you, and/or men with unresolved substance abuse issues (unresolved means not in a program or in counseling). These people are the way they are. You can't change them or save them, and they can't change for you. People don't generally change without a lot of work. If the ship is sinking, get off before you go down, too. Your time is precious and your life is worth more. Plus, if you don't work through the relationship and learn from it, you'll probably have to repeat this scenario with another unavailable person. No thanks.

This baggage-removal exercise can make you feel like Spirit is conspiring against you by challenging you with temptations similar to those in your past. You break it off with one unavailable man only to wind up in a relationship with another more cunningly disguised unavailable man. You think that if he is unable or unwilling to give you what you want, it doesn't mean he's wrong for you. It just means that he may be wrong for you today.

If you keep finding yourself with people that can't seem to commit, consider that you may be, on some level, attracting these people on purpose. Stay with us here. Just consider that you may be attracting these people because you are meant to work through your own commitment issues. Therapy is great for helping you work this out, and/or you can try this exercise below.

Write a note to Mr. Unavailable. No need to send it. Knowing we won't send it can sometimes make us more honest. If you still hold a lot of negative emotion toward someone, keep writing to this person until you feel more relieved than angry.

- First, tell them how you think they wronged you.

- Second, tell them exactly what you liked about being with them (have fun!). Know that all the fun you had with them you are utterly capable of experiencing with another.

> *Lie to me, I promise to believe. Lie to me, but please don't leave.*
> *—Sheryl Crow*

- Third, tell them you know they were doing the best they could (even if that was far from good enough), and tell them you are letting them off the hook. You don't have to feel they deserve to be let off the hook, but you do have to feel like you've let yourself off the hook and that you don't have to hold on to it anymore.

- Finally, burn the letter and vow to yourself not to continue relationships with people who are unable to love you. As it burns, bless your future lover and tell the universe you are ready to receive new, available love.

Here's an example:

Dear Ian,

I forgive you. I know you did the best you could at the time. Even if that meant stomping on the tender heart I handed you over and over again. Even though you weren't able to love me fully. I could have been a better partner, too. Were you trying to tell me something by cheating on me and dumping me over and over again? Anyway . . . we had a lot of fun, but I'm glad we're not together anymore. If ever I felt you owed me anything, I don't anymore. I'm moving on. Thanks for everything I've learned from dating you. I had so much fun with you.

Truly all the best,
Marni

PS I hope you don't age well, and you get in deep trouble with one of the married women you like to cheat with. Bwah-ha-ha-ha!

Day 13 Exercise: Establish Boundaries with Vampire Friends

Vampire friends are those that suck the energy out of you. When they call, you tire immediately and want to hang up. Maybe their task in your life is to test your boundaries, and your task with them is to assert yourself.

> *Lisa, vampires are make-believe, like elves, gremlins, and eskimos.*
> —Homer Simpson

Clearly asserting your boundaries will show them what you will or won't tolerate. For example, when a vampire friend calls, state at the beginning of the conversation how much time you have to talk. "Hey Joe, nice to hear from you. I've got fifteen minutes to chat, then I have to go. What's up?" Joe will be happy because he has fifteen minutes of your attention, and you'll be happy because you've given Joe your boundary of how much time you have to chat. You're not allowing him to take up more time and energy than you have or want to give. Be sure to stick with the boundary you've set. Interestingly, vampire friends seem to overstep boundaries and suck all the air out of the room.

If you're in the mood, feel free to even coss them off your list—permanently—and give your energy to friends who support you instead.

Day 14: Procrastination, 'Cause I've Got All Day

The gift turned inward, unable to be given, becomes
a heavy burden, even sometimes a kind of poison.
It is as though the flow of life were back up.
—May Sarton

The long, long journey of procrastination usually starts with many stops at what we call the Can't Stop Café. At the Can't Stop Café we sidle up to the bar, ask the waitress for a black coffee, which she delivers in a white diner cup, and begin a diatribe about how we "coulda been somebody" if only we had followed through.

Whenever we can't stop doing something, it's usually because unconscious impulses are pulling us away from what we truly want in life. No matter how little these "can't stop" tendencies seem to be, they are not insignificant and they are not meaningless. Most often they are caused by competing intentions. On the one hand, our conscious mind wants us to go out and be the best we can be. On the other, our subconscious may feel most at home in shame and fear because that is what we are used to feeling. The confusion these "can't stop" tendencies generate causes us to procrastinate and put off doing those things that will bring us what we want in life.

Here are some "can't stop" examples:

- Can't stop being shy around cute people.
- Can't say goodbye to . . .
- Can't get rid of . . .
- Can't "quit you."
- Can't get off my couch to go out.
- Can't stop eating sweets every day even though I want to quit eating sugar.
- Can't seem to lose five pounds.
- Can't stop cheating even though I love my mate.
- Can't seem to get it together.
- Can't seem to grow up.
- Can't stop procrastinating.

When we are controlled by procrastination and "can't stop" thoughts, the unconscious desires at work are usually stronger than the desire to stop. These desires are linked to much deeper stuff like the need to feel bad about ourselves, to feel chunkier than we want to be in order to feel safe, to feel like a liar, to feel "dirty," to be irresponsible, to be right, to blame the world for not giving us a break. Until we start looking at these impulses, it may be hard to stop procrastinating and truly achieve our goals.

Day 14 Exercise: Stop Procrastinating

There is always something we put off because it makes us feel uncomfortable. If only it were as easy as just doing it. Procrastination is powerful. It is so powerful that it can keep us from achieving our dreams. It can keep us from having a great love life. It can keep us from feeling the warm light of Spirit that is always upon us. Seriously. Procrastination can wreck everything. Stupid procrastination. And most often procrastination is just fear. Stupid fear.

Marni had a beautiful poetry teacher in college. One day he asked her why she wasn't writing as much as she used to. "I guess I've just been lazy," she said. "There is no such thing as lazy, only fear," he said. It stuck with her and she started writing again.

Consider something you may be procrastinating about, like say, oh we don't know . . . throwing out those old love letters. Or maybe taking care of your taxes in order to get your finances under control. Could you possibly be avoiding letting go of unhealthy vampire friends? Perhaps you have an addiction you want to get under control but have yet to make it to a twelve-step meeting. Could it possibly be an exercise from days 4 through 17 that you are putting off? If so, here are four ways to help you stop procrastinating:

1. **Go to a therapist or life coach.** You may need someone outside of yourself who can oversee your challenges from a neutral position. When you're in the midst of a battle, you need to discover what you're fighting. You can't slay your enemy until you drag it into the light and recognize it for what it is. The help of a good counselor is invalable.

2. **Be accountable.** Find someone you would not want to let down. Someone that lives the kind of life you want to live. Share your procrastination struggles and ask if you can check in with them as a way of being accountable for your actions.

3. **Start keeping small commitments to yourself.** There is tremendous power in the ability to keep commitments to yourself. Start with small ones, then move on up to bigger ones. Don't make a commitment to yourself if you're not going to keep it. If you make a list of ten items and only get three done, you could feel like you've let yourself down. But if you make a list of ten items and tell yourself you're committed to getting done the most important three and anything else on the list is gravy, then you've kept a commitment to yourself instead of letting yourself down.

4. **Procrastinate by procrastinating.** Huh? Avoid doing one activity by doing another activity you've been avoiding.For example, Janice has three things she was constantly procrastinating about: exercise, looking for a job, and doing homework. So if she didn't want to exercise, she looked for a job. If she didn't want to look for a job, she did her homework. If she didn't want to do her homework, she exercised. Try it. It works!

Day 15: Make a Decision and Stick to It

Until a person can say deeply and honestly, "I am what
I am today because of the choice I made yesterday,"
that person cannot say, "I choose otherwise."
—Stephen Covey, author

Now that we've learned what it takes to stop procrastinating and start getting things done, we have freed up some time and energy. This means we can make a decision to get out there and do something about having the love we want. Real change requires decision making. Such decisions can be very easy to renege on, especially if you start to feel uncomfortable once you take action. Then you can bet your subconscious will soon want you to quit. Here are some tips to keep your subconscious at bay and help you make a decision and stick to it:

- **Keep Perspective.** Emotions cloud judgment, so cool off before you make a big decision. If you feel like you have to *do* something, give it a day to see if you still feel it's necessary. Don't make decisions based on what you stand to lose. Look at what you stand to gain and stay focused on the prize. Maybe even do a pros and cons list, which, though we realize is a pain in the arse, can give you some perspective.

- **Set long-term goals.** How does what you're doing right now fit into your big picture? Does it get you what you really want? Does having a long-distance relationship that's going nowhere even though you really love each other get you closer to living in the same town? Do you still want to be having phone sex in five years? Look at the long term. Do you have a plan or do you just hope it all falls into place? The hope approach is passive and not proactive.

- **Listen to your gut.** Studies have shown that the instinctual gut reaction people feel upon meeting a stranger usually proves correct 90 percent of the time so don't dismiss what your gut has to say even if you don't like what it's saying.

- **Ask for help from the right people.** Endless input won't help you reach your goals. Don't ask everyone and their dog what they think, just ask trusted friends that have some experience with what you want to know about. Opinions are like brains, everyone has one, though some are more enlightened than others. But not everyone has experience. When you want advice, ask someone knowledgeable.

- **Quit obsessing.** Worrying about making the perfect decision just wastes time and sprouts gray hair. It doesn't get you closer to your destination. People who are successful decision makers make the "good enough" decision and move on.

- **Don't second-guess.** Accept your choice because you can't know the full impact of a decision until time has passed anyway. You did the research, you asked opinions, you listened to your gut. There will always be a degree of uncertainty, so relax. You did well.

- **Take stock.** It's important to gauge how your decisions are affecting your life. Sometimes we are unaware of the progress we are actually making. For example, Janice was feeling like her love life wasn't exactly where it should be, but then she looked for places in her day were she had great love in her life, and she was able to shift her perspective and see the good. Here's one of her journal entries:.

Reasons why I had great love in my life today:

1. Saw Marni and she said I had great cheekbones.

2. Guy at the computer store sympathized with my frustrations and made my return fast and easy.

3. Saw one of my neighbors walking her puppy, and I played with him.

4. Saturday morning crew at the coffee shop found me a chair so I could sit and enjoy my coffee.

5. Kirk saw me walking, picked me up, and drove me to yoga. We shared his Twizzlers and laughed.

6. In yoga, my body was able to hold the balance poses better.

7. Had yummy chai tea with Dana and we giggled about nothing much, which is the most fun thing to giggle about.

8. Read a beautiful description of how in Saskatchewan you can watch the wind make waves in the wheat.

9. Noticed how my messy pile of papers is finally going down. Feeling like I'm on my way to getting it together.

10. Lay down for bed and had to get up and write down one idea that turned into five, and it solved a section of the piece I've been writing, which means I'm one step closer to the piece being realized!!!

Day 15 Exercise: Be Grateful

Gratitude is the true path to abundance. When Spirit sees we are grateful and can easily handle the love we already have in our life, we are given more. So in order to have abundant loving lives, start by being grateful for what love you currently have. From now until the end of the thirty days, you're going to make a list of at least ten reasons you have great love in your life. The items on your list can be as big as "I love how my mom called today just when I needed to hear a friendly voice" to something as seemingly little as "I love the candy jar at reception." Yum, we love the candy jar, too.

Part 3
Creative Fantasizing

Day 16: Tap In to the Creative Vortex

There is a vitality, a life force, an energy, a quickening that is translated through you into action and because there is only one of you in all of time, this expression is unique. And if you block it, it will never exist through any other medium and be lost.
—Martha Graham, dancer

In "Remove Baggage" we cleaned out a lot of personal and material stuff. Over time, the working through of personal issues and the removal of material baggage will help you to let go of any inner baggage you may still be carrying around. The same goes for these next three days: when you start making inner changes in the way you think and act, delightful outer changes will come accordingly.

What Is the Creative Vortex?

A single gal asking a happily married woman how she knew her husband was The One often gets the same irritating answer: "I just knew." Yeah. Uh, we single folks want some concrete answers here and "just knowing" isn't good enough. But the inner voice that spoke to them and gave them the gut reaction of just knowing came from a place we call the Creative Vortex. It is where gut reactions and senses of destiny and "just knowing" originate from. It's the wise inner voice that talks to you and says good things such as "Go up to him! Go up to him!" and sometimes says uncomfortable things such as "You have to be the one to leave this relationship" or "You are settling here because you are scared you can't do better." Ouch.

> *If we choose to passively wait for that ideal boyfriend to appear in our living room, we may wait a long, long time.*

Our challenge is to tap in to the Creative Vortex, which means trusting our gut and listening to our inner voice even when it tells us to move on when we want to stay. Luckily, it is fun to start tapping in to the Creative Vortex. We start by writing, painting, taking photos, and creating anew.

> *One does not "find oneself" by pursuing one's self, but on the contrary by pursuing something else and learning through discipline or routine . . . who one is and wants to be.*
> —May Sarton, author

Even If You Don't Feel Creative, You Are

> *We choose our joys and sorrows long before we experience them.*
> —Kahlil Gibran

Even if you have never been musical or artistic or never liked to read, you are creative. There is not one human being that is not creative. It is part of our human makeup. We are creating every minute. Even if you are just watching TV, you are creating for yourself a moment of watching TV. Some of us tap into creativity more easily than others, but we are each highly creative every day in the sense that we create our lives as we go along—no one is following a script. We get to watch our lives unfold day by day before us. Everything we think about, believe, assume, and do is part of our creative process. We are all creative works in progress.

Sometimes, we get hung up on our "work in progress." Complacency sets in, and we start thinking that since the future we want is already waiting for us out there, we need do nothing but sit back and wait for the day to come. News flash: Today is the day. When we know what we want, we can ask Spirit for assistance in creating our destiny. However, if we don't actively create what we want, we live life in a reactive way instead of a proactive way. We tumble along until eventually, we fall into something sticky.

We Create Who We Want to Be, What We Want to Have, and What We Deserve

> *If you limit your choices to what seems possible or reasonable, you disconnect yourself from what you truly want, and all that is left is compromise.*
> —Robert Fritz

If we truly believe we are undeserving of a great love life, then we don't get a great love life because we manifest what we believe. That's why if you find you are in a cycle of negative, self-defeating, thinking patterns, it is very important to learn how to shift them. We are not saying it is a piece of cake, but we are saying you can create whatever you want through your thoughts. Ever have people tell you they deserve better or you deserve better? You don't usually get what you deserve, you get what you *think* you deserve. For example, if you think there are no good men out there, you may have a tougher time finding yourself a good man. Your thoughts become you, so be aware of what you think.

The Creative Vortex listens to our requests and gives us back what we tell it we want. It doesn't argue. It fulfills our desires. It is very accommodating. Ask for and work toward what you *really* want.

Janice's Charmed Life

Ever since I decided to recite to myself, "I have a charmed life," magical things have happened. People call just when I was thinking about them. I run into someone who tells me something random that helps me through a situation. I desire something as complex as a new apartment or something as minute as cool fridge magnets and immediately the best apartment is put on the market, I scoop it up, and a friend gives me fridge magnets as a housewarming gift. I live a charmed life because I told the Creative Vortex that I wanted to. It's super easy and the results are astounding.

Day 16 Exercise: Create a Comfort Station

A comfort station is a place where you can dream. It's where you can go to get away from the hustle bustle of every day, lie down, and fantasize. The only requirement of this station is that it be a place where you won't be interrupted, so you can let your mind wander. You may choose to carve out a corner of your bedroom by putting pillows and a lamp on the floor. One of our friends set up a camping tent (a comfort fort!) in the corner of her living room where she could go to dream, paint, and drink tea. Another friend doesn't have a physical space set up in his house, but he has a box of art supplies that he brings out so he can draw or paint at his kitchen table. In this box, he even has a secret stash of butter rum Lifesavers and a special mug that he uses to make tea during this time. When he's done with his session, he can easily pack up his portable comfort station.

Whatever type of comfort station you create, you'll want it to be a place that has a good vibe where you can really let yourself feel free. And you'll be visiting it all the time so make sure it's in an accessible place.

Here's a list of Creative Vortex supplies you may want to have in your comfort station:

- Journal
- Favorite writing pen
- Drawing paper—printer paper will do
- Markers
- Colored pencils
- Crayons
- Watercolors (cheap ones from the drugstore are great)
- Scissors
- Magazines
- Glue/Glue stick
- Glitter/Glitter glue
- Music
- Snacks
- Whatever you want!

Every day when you sit down in your comfort station, repeat the following sentence five times. It's a nice warm-up to doing the activities in this book, and it helps call in Spirit to assist you in attracting love into your life. After you've recited the sentence, spend ten minutes fantasizing about loving and being loved by your future lover.

I am ready and open to love and be loved. I easily accept my beautiful self. I am amazing right now. I have a charmed life. My light is always shining.

    We copied this sentence on a card and pinned it in our comfort stations for easy reference. Feel free to copy it down, decorate it with images that call to you, color it, paint it, and get really creative with it.

> *If you hear a voice within you say, "you cannot paint," then by all means paint and that voice will be silenced.*
>
> —*Vincent Van Gogh*

Days 17 & 18: Call In the Creative Muse

"Do or do not, there is no try."
—Yoda

Some believe they need to be in love or recently out of love in order to be creative. It's as if they need a muse to muster the creative muscle. Sure, these are definitely inspired times and they make for great material, but how do we become creative *in order to attract love into our life* when it feels like there is nothing creative happening?

What If You Don't Feel Creative Anymore?

You used to be so creative. You used to be inspired. You used to paint and stay up late writing poetry. You used to play your guitar all the time and sing and compose in your head. Now you just lug your guitar from sublet to sublet and never actually play it. You save all your old journals from the good old prolific days, and you plan on keeping them for when you write a brilliant book someday. You still jot down scraps of song or poetry on napkins or receipts to save for the day that the muse hits again. Eventually the scraps get thrown away. You may even feel bad when you trash them, and you vow to get back into being creative and inspired some day soon. But in the meantime, you just don't want to deal. Your plate is full and yet you feel like you are starving.

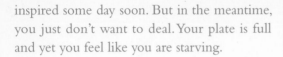

Einstein's definition of insanity: Doing the same thing over and over and expecting different results.

Ponder When You Were Creative

Were you creative in school? You may have finished school eons ago and perhaps aren't in the routine of writing, drawing, and fantasizing anymore. You no longer have Creative Writing, Photography, band practice, or even lunch time to hang with your friends, lie in the grass, and dream. These days, because you don't have creative assignments due, you have little motivation to be creative. Back in school, the "doing it" and "getting it done" part was apparently all it took to conjure the muse. Now, you have *real work* to do. It's all rather draining and by the time the work is done, you don't want to expend any more creative energy on anything. You just want to watch TV and go to bed.

Creative Juicing Idea

Need a push to get the creativity flowing? Take a class. Look up the course listings of local schools to find a class that calls to you. You could take a class in art, photography, writing, acting, swimming, or even in creativity itself. They offer those, too.

You may even wonder if your creative side exists anymore. Did it atrophy like a tricycle left out in the rain for good? You may mourn that something that was once a frustrating and wonderful distraction is not important anymore. You have a job, stuff to do, and *responsibilities*. No time to get on that bike again. Besides, you have a car.

> *When you do things from your soul, you feel a river moving in you, a joy. When actions come from another section, the feeling disappears.*
> —Rumi

Being Creative Is in the Doing

> *When your life is oh so dreary, dream.*
> —Smashing Pumpkins

As the saying goes: If you do what you've always done, you'll get what you've always got. You can read tons of books on the subject of meditation, and you can lament about not doing it because you don't know how, or it doesn't work for you, or you just don't get it. But until you plop down to breathe for ten minutes, you're not going to know how it goes.

When you were a kid, you didn't care what jobs made money or gave prestige. You just knew firemen slid down poles, jump ropes had many uses, and anyone could be a superhero. You spent lazy afternoons in the yard seriously looking for fairies and four-leaf clovers. All this time, you're brain was naturally creative. It didn't have any rules about what was possible and what wasn't.

You knew the art of letting yourself be. You still have the same brain. The creative part is still there. It just needs to be brought out.

No Need to Do It Perfectly

The point of creative activities is not to learn how to beat yourself up better or give yourself one more thing to say you're doing wrong. We want to help you learn and grow. The activities are done to facilitate you letting go of things that don't propel you forward and to teach you to embrace and enlarge the things that do. There is no wrong way to do any creative endeavor. If we tell you to cut out magazine pictures and you want to draw, write a poem, or paint every day, do what works for you. As long as your activity is in keeping with the integrity of where we are moving toward, feel free to . . . well, be creative.

Why Do I Have to Be Creative to Have a Great Love Life?

Being creative helps us tap into the Creative Vortex mentioned earlier, which helps attract more love into our lives and helps us read intuitive messages from Spirit, which lead us in the best direction. Creativity is a muscle that can be worked just like any other in your body. The more you let yourself be free and creative, the more you will come to trust yourself in other areas. Being creative can sometimes bring up self-doubt and self-judgment. Don't look at it as a bad thing. Look at it as a blessing that these issues are coming up to be healed.

Maybe you won't like what you've created, and you'll want to quit and never do it again. But keep doing it. The beauty is in the act of doing it rather than in the result. Let go of needing to be perfect or even good. For every one masterpiece there may be twenty duds. It's all good. Just be nice to yourself through the learning process. Sooner or later you'll learn to trust your creative choices. You'll learn that it doesn't have to be perfect, that you don't even have to like it. We begin to realize that we are doing it for pleasure, not for some outcome. As you grow more free and accepting of yourself, your beauty will grow, too, and you will be freer, happier, and sexier.

The Creative Vortex propels you to go to the places you are meant to be and meet the people you are meant to meet. When you create art or write poetry, the hunches and nudges and words

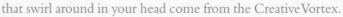

that swirl around in your head come from the Creative Vortex. They are clues telling you where to go next. Learning how to hear and trust this voice will help attract soul mates. Besides, like we said, a by-product of creativity is feeling more sexy and free. Plus, you'll look brighter and happier, which also makes you more attractive.

Creative acts are an expression of love for ourselves that we are offering to the Universe even if no one sees the product. It's a gift just to let ourselves be a channel for birthing something new into this world. See where your process takes you.

Days 17 & 18 Exercises: Free Your Creativity

Head to your comfort station and do a few of these activities. There is no way to do them wrong. The only requirement is a desire to have fun and free your creativity without judgment.

- **Do what you loved in third grade.** If you loved to write, look up an old journal entry and from it, create a poem, even if you feel like it is the worst poem ever. No one is reading it but you anyway, right? If you loved to paint or thought you might, buy paints from the children's section at the drugstore and finger paint to 80s music.

If you sniffed glue, make a collage of images from magazines and interesting paper you've collected around town. We love old diner receipts, guitar repair tags, and playing cards. There need not be a theme to this collage. Let the theme, if any, arise as you do it. Its inspiration is based on the interesting images you've collected.

If you loved playing soccer at recess, find (or purchase) a soccer ball and do some drills. You can even dribble around your house or look for a pickup game in your neighborhood.

- **Yell and scream.** Swear like a drunken sailor. Act like an offshoreman with Tourettes. Do it loud and do it proud. Or if no words come, moan and groan and make it come from the bottom of your belly. This helps shake creativity out of dormancy. The sounds that come out may make you laugh. You may want to find a private place for this one. We like the inside of our cars. They are mobile comfort stations. We also scream in our bedrooms if no one is around.

- **Memorize a scene from your favorite movie.** *The Godfather* is great for this. *Good Fellas,* too. "What? You think I'm funny? You think I'm a f★★★ing clown?" Not only is memorizing a scene exercising your creative muscle, you can use it at dinner parties, too.

- **Do a modern dance.** Stay with us on this one. It's really fun once we get over how silly we may feel about it. Head to your comfort station, play any song you love, close your eyes, and move your body. Move in ways you possibly wouldn't dare if you were at a dance club. Let yourself feel the music and shake up the still areas of your body. Marni's favorite is "Linus and Lucy" from the *Charlie Brown Christmas* album.

- **Carve out silent moments.** In the noise of daily life, we literally cannot hear ourselves think. Give your brain a break from taking in all the sights and sounds of the day and let your mind wander. Take a quiet tea break and stare into oblivion. If you have a hard time just sitting, close your eyes and take ten breaths. Lie flat on your back and stare at the ceiling. You can also do this activity at work every day this week. Sit in a bathroom stall for an extra minute and just breathe. Bathroom stalls are little comfort stations where you can carve out a quick moment, and they are everywhere!

Day 19: Get Clear by Creating Your Dream List

Just don't give up trying to do what you really want to do.
Where there is love and inspiration, I don't think you can go wrong.
—Ella Fitzgerald

Now that we've warmed up the creative muscles, we can dig in and get clarity on what we want out of our great love lives. After all, how are we going to find what we want when we don't know exactly what it is? In the next few sections, we will be defining what we want from our love lives so that when we get out there we can recognize all the love that will be staring us in the face.

Proactive vs. Reactive

We have a much higher chance of creating what we want when we are proactive. Proactivity means we anticipate what we want and go after it rather than sit back and react to what comes our way. When we are clear about what we want, we can then take actions to make it happen. Yet, so often we live reactive lives, spending all our time and energy reacting to what comes at us and juggling it as fast as we can. Then one day we wake up and realize we are on a path we did not want.

How to Proactively Create a Relationship

High expectations of others leads to disappointments, but personally creating what we want in our own lives leads to empowerment and satisfaction.

Imagine that you are sick. Your nose runs, you feel achy, and your head hurts. You probably take medicine to numb your aches or dry up your nose. You think that the runny nose, aches, and pains are the problem because they are the parts of you that hurt most immediately. In reality, if we wanted to get sick a lot less often, we would realize that the problem was not our aches or runny nose; it was that the cold virus festered more easily because our immune systems may have been run down and we needed to get more sleep, eat better, and drink more water. It is just easier to treat the symptoms of the problem than taking steps to avoid the problem itself. Treating the problem of overall health would take ongoing effort and lifestyle shifts, and lets face it, it's easier to take a pill.

The same goes for relationships. We think that the problem is the other person. If only they would rise to our expectations, everyone would get along just fine. Perhaps our expectations aren't even that high, or we read meaning into things—he doesn't put the seat down, so he's not thinking of me; he doesn't remember to get my groceries at the market, only his own, so he is selfish; he doesn't want to come to my friend's wedding with me, so he doesn't care about me. Is the problem really him or is it our expectation of him to make us happy?

Chances are, it's the latter. So how do you proactively create a relationship you really want? Don't expect to necessarily change him or find someone different. Instead, take care of yourself and keep bringing the focus back to you. When you shift the focus onto yourself instead of him, everything shifts for the better. If you spend your time liking yourself rather than wondering how to make him like you more, you'll be much farther ahead and more fully engaged in the world. And when you make the decision to personally create what you want and do the necessary footwork to bring it to you, you can avoid a lot of disappointment.

We spend a lot of time unsure of what we want and then feel disappointed and resigned when nothing comes to us. But we are the ones that create our lives so when we are unsure, the results we get are murky. Even blaming someone else for what has happened in our lives is our creation because we control what we do and how we react. This is important enough to mention again: *We are responsible for everything that happens in our lives because we control what we do and how we react.* If we envision ourselves being upset, chances are we will get upset. If we envision ourselves happy and calm, chances are greater that we will be happy and calm.

When Marni was dating David and discovered he cheated on her, she decided to stay with him. She loved him, and he said it was "just sex" with the other woman, not love. But when he cheated on her again, she berated herself for staying with him. She wanted to blame him, but she knew that ultimately she was responsible because she chose to stay with a man who betrayed her. She could not blame him and make it all his fault. She had to wonder what made her stay and why she was so unwilling to give up on him. She had to decide if she was really okay with dating someone who cheats on her because clearly David had shown her that he would cheat on her again and again. Ultimately, she didn't want to leave him because she was afraid of losing his "love," but she knew she could no longer blame him for her pain because she was the one who chose to stay. After their tumultuous breakup she realized she had "needed" his love because she wasn't giving herself love. As she slowly worked on giving to herself, she no longer needed him.

Creating a Healthy Relationship with Ourselves

On a deeper level, the issues in our relationships with others are only mirroring back to us our relationships with ourselves. Most of the time, the other person is not aware of your personal challenges and, what's more, they have no idea

> *Cheat on me and break up with me once, shame on you. Cheat on me and break up with me four times, are you trying to tell me something?*

what you're thinking. If we consistently find ourselves having a hard time maintaining loving, giving, and committed relationships, then we have to ask ourselves what is going on in our relationship with ourselves. For Marni, it would have been more productive to evaluate whether she had a hard time being loving, giving, and committed to herself, rather than blame David for not being more committed to her. We all grow, learn, and process at different rates. The best thing we can do is be open to looking in the proverbial mirror.

When we ourselves are healthy, we attract healthy people. When we work on creating a healthy relationship with ourselves, we are dealing with the root of the problem instead of just trying to get rid of the symptoms. We will attract different people and our challenging relationships with others will shift as well. When we take care of ourselves physically (eating the right foods, drinking in moderation, getting enough exercise), mentally (stimulating and challenging ourselves, being creative), and emotionally and spiritually (having a support system, knowing to seek help when we need it), we can be loving and committed to ourselves and attract healthier relationships.

You have the ability to create whatever you want in your life. Dream big. Don't wait for anyone else to give you a break. Come through for yourself. That famous book *The Rules* emphasizes that we should *act* busy to give the illusion that we have a full and exciting life in order to attract the good man. Here's a fresh idea: *have* a full and exciting life.

Day 19 Exercise A: Make a Dream List

You are going to get clear about what you want by creating a Dream List. Now this list will be of things *you* want. Not something that you think other people want for you. It's very important to be honest about what you want for yourself.

Make a list of what you want to accomplish in life. Be creative. It can include activities you haven't done in years or things you haven't done yet at all. Stretch your imagination here. You only have to make your dreams 50 percent believable. These are not supposed to be lists of things you *have* to do. Rather, make a list of the way you want your life to be. So rather than write, "Exercise three times a week," change it to "Enjoy my consistent workouts." Also, you don't want to be dependent on someone else to fulfill the items on your list. If you have "Become valedictorian," you could change it to "Be the best student I can be." You can stretch the dream, too.

If you are currently out of shape but want a toned, flexible body, then say, "Love my awesome, healthy, and toned body." Of course, you're a babe in our eyes no matter what.

Marni's and Janice's Dream List Example:

- Do a paint-by-numbers while listening to my favorite CD
- Ride a beach cruiser
- Teach creativity classes and feel alive and inspired in them
- Write in a fancy cliff-side hotel in Big Sur
- Make candy-cane martinis
- Make a tiara out of sea glass
- Lie in bed and let my mind drift more often
- Break out the glitter and paints and get messy
- Memorize a poem
- Have coffee on Saturday mornings with my lover
- Drive up the coast
- Learn to surf
- Get my ex out of my head
- Burn the ex's love letters
- Find my dream house and easily buy it
- Paint a painting, frame it, and give it to a friend
- Easily afford a massage every month

- Wear matching bra and panties much more often
- Cook stress-free, nutritional meals for my family
- Have lovely children
- Marry my best friend and lover
- Publish an article that makes a positive change
- Ride in the mountains on the back of a motorcycle
- Learn to speak French fluently
- Go up the Eiffel Tower
- Attend more book signings
- See more live music
- Take an advanced guitar class and not be lost
- Appreciate my flexible, toned, strong body
- Spend an abundant fun year in New York City with someone I love
- Have a kick-ass brownie recipe that I pass down to my children

Day 19 Exercise B: Make a Things I Love to Do List

- Read the paper on the weekend
- Take bubble baths
- Lie in the sun
- Drink coffee at Peet's

- Pick up shells at the beach
- Bake cookies
- Watch live music
- Make jewelry
- Go rollerblading

Now review this list and check off any you may have already done this past month. If you haven't checked off much, ask yourself if you are doing what you love often enough. If not, make a point this week of doing some of the activities on this list.

Brownie Recipe *(cont'd on the next page)*

If you're in the market for a brownie recipe worthy of passing down to your future kids with stories of how you made them to effectively make their father fall in love with you, here is one that is super chocolatey, dense, and has that delectable crackly top.

6 ounces semisweet chocolate
½ cup (1 stick) unsalted butter
2 large eggs
1 cup granulated sugar
1 tablespoon unsweetened cocoa powder
1 teaspoon vanilla extract
1 teaspoon brewed espresso (or really rich coffee)
¾ teaspoon salt
1 cup all-purpose flour

Preheat oven to 350°F. Line a 8x8 baking pan with parchment paper.

In a saucepan over medium-low heat, stir the chocolate and butter together until melted. Remove from heat and set aside to cool to nearly room temperature.

Mix together the eggs, sugar, cocoa powder, vanilla extract, espresso and salt. Add the cooled chocolate and mix. Fold in the flour just until incorporated.

Turn into baking dish and bake 25 to 30 minutes, until a tester comes out clean. Cool completely before cutting.

Yields: We don't know because we cut them really small, so we can have two instead of one.

Day 20: Commit to Your Dream

You must ask for what you really want.
—Rumi

Are you commitment phobic? If your answer goes something like, "Pahlease! It's not *me* who has the commitment issues, it's *him*. I have no problems with commitment," then we ask you to take a good, honest look at how you live your life on a daily basis. Take Alanna for example. She's not sinking. She's not swimming. She's staying above water. She's maintaining the status quo. Sure, she's committed to her job, staying current with news events, and keeping in touch with friends. When we interviewed her and asked her to create a Dream list, among her top items were to go back to school for a higher degree, to publish a children's book she had already written a few years ago, and to be fluent in French. She also wanted to be dating her future husband within the next three years. When we asked her about the time she's taking for herself to accomplish some of the goals on her list her response was, "I don't have time to make time for myself. I'm too busy earning money, keeping up friendships, paying my bills, keeping my house clean, keeping up my social life. I'm too tired to work toward my goals when I'm done with everything else." Here's a look at Alanna's daily routines.

Alanna's Daily Routine List

- Wake up at 8:00
- Watch twenty minutes of TV
- Get ready
- Drive to work and listen to NPR
- Be at work at 9:30
- Work all day/e-mail with friends
- Get home at 5:30
- Prepare dinner
- Talk on the phone
- Surf the Net
- Watch TV
- Go to bed

Alanna's Weekend

- Sleep in
- Make coffee and read the paper
- Do errands around town (tailor, dry cleaner, laundry, car wash, shoe store, etc.)
- Go to dinner and a movie with a friend

All these little "things to do" had kept Alanna at a distance from what she really wanted. Her actions weren't in line with her goals. None of her activities involved working toward her dreams. And these unmet dreams were draining her energy. That's why she felt unfulfilled. What happened to the children's book? The French classes? The love life? When she compared her Dream list to her Daily Routine list, she realized she wasn't currently committed to her dreams. "Hello. My name is Alanna and I am commitment phobic." Often, we think we'll do all that fun stuff when we have more time. Then time passes and more time never comes.

We asked Alanna to pick one of her goals. She decided to learn French. That week, she bought French tapes to play in the car, and she signed up for a class at the city college. Just doing that made her feel more satisfied with how her life was evolving. Going to class was also in line with her goal of meeting others who shared her interests.

Here's how our friend Wendy took a tiny step toward fulfilling her goal of meeting a cute boy.

I make coffee at home because it's easy. But my goal on my Dream list was to meet a cute boy. So I decided to make

> *Whatever you can do or dream you can, begin it. Boldness has genius, power and magic in it. Begin it now.*
> —Goethe

one small change in my daily life. How was I to meet a cute boy when I am not getting out? I chose to go out to Peet's Coffee & Tea for coffee in the morning instead of making it at home. At first I was resistant because I like the time alone at home to think. However, I realized from my Daily Routine list that I had plenty of time alone. So I started going to the same coffee shop at the same time every morning. Going there repeatedly helped me warm up to the other people who went there at the same time day after day. At one point, a really cute guy struck up a conversation with me. We started to have small chit chats every morning. Nothing happened romantically, but it was fun to go out and flirt a little over coffee before work. He kind of became a lure to get me to keep going to Peet's for coffee. I met more people. Eventually I did start dating someone—the barista! What a story to tell my kids. We have so much fun together, and I am so glad I made that one little change in my daily life. It's made all the difference in the world.

Because Wendy was committed to the goal of meeting someone, even this small act of going out for coffee set in motion a divine power and it seemed the Universe conspired to help her achieve her goals. All sorts of serendipitous events started to happen that would never have otherwise occurred had she not set her intention to meet someone and changed one little aspect of her daily life.

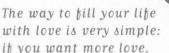

> *The way to fill your life with love is very simple: if you want more love, give more love.*
> —Deepak Chopra

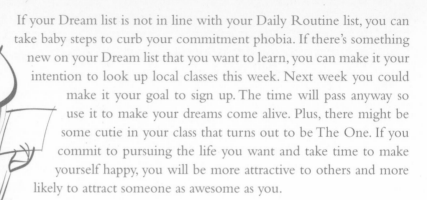

If your Dream list is not in line with your Daily Routine list, you can take baby steps to curb your commitment phobia. If there's something new on your Dream list that you want to learn, you can make it your intention to look up local classes this week. Next week you could make it your goal to sign up. The time will pass anyway so use it to make your dreams come alive. Plus, there might be some cutie in your class that turns out to be The One. If you commit to pursuing the life you want and take time to make yourself happy, you will be more attractive to others and more likely to attract someone as awesome as you.

Day 20 Exercise: Make a Daily Routine List

Go to your comfort station, grab a pen and paper, and make a quick list of what you really do with your time. Review your list, then look back at your Dream list from the previous chapter. Are any of the activities you do on a daily basis contributing to achieving your dreams on your Dream list? If not, this week take one action in your daily life that contributes to achieving one goal on your Dream list. For example, if you put on your Dream list that you wanted to spend a weekend with friends in a cabin in the woods, an action step you take in your daily life may be to research cabin rentals.

Another action step could be to book time off work with the intention of using that time to go to the cabin. It doesn't matter how big or small your action step is. What matters is that you commit to doing it, and you fulfill this commitment. This tells Spirit that you value yourself and are ready to be with someone who values you.

We attract what we are.

Day 21: Create a Lover List

There are four questions of value in life . . . What is sacred?
Of what is the spirit made? What is worth living for, and what
is worth dying for? The answer to each is the same. Only love.
—Johnny Depp in Don Juan de Marco

Man oh man, don't we just love lists! The Lover list helps us describe the type of person we want in our great love life so the Creative Vortex can go out and help find him on our behalf. Seriously. How great is that?! Soon you will make a list of what you want in a lover. The purpose of the list is to get you excited about having what you really want. It's a way to clarify your own intention. After all, if you don't know what you want, how will you attract it? And how will the Creative Vortex know what to look for? Make it somewhat believable, but let yourself fantasize even if you don't think it entirely possible. We're not telling you that just by writing the list you will magically manifest Mr. Perfect. That's a bit New Agey even for us. But it will help you clarify what is important to you in a lover. Plus, the power of intention can be pretty magical.

Don't be afraid to admit what you are looking for on your list. If you know that you want to be in a committed monogamous relationship heading on a straight path for marriage, it is okay to communicate that on your list. You need not be afraid of being too forward or scaring anyone away. This is your list, and you want to eventually find someone who wants similar things. There are plenty of people out there just like you. Keep your list in the present tense as if everything you already want has been put in motion. Try to make your list more attuned to feelings than material specifics. For example, instead of "I am sitting in our living room with my new husband, Brad," say, "I am so happy to be comfortable in our living room with my awesome husband who is as hot for me as I am for him."

Looking for love is a profound way to stretch and grow yourself emotionally. In the search for true love, the best, the worst, and the most horrifyingly immature may be brought out in us. It is possible for dating to suck big time, but if you look at it as a gift to self—like going back to school to learn more about who you are—it can be a tool to help you bring out the best version of yourself.

Know Who You Are and What You Want

The point of dating is to find a partner that is equally committed to learning and growing with you. It is our natural instinct to grow and change and learn. It is also a natural instinct to go through life two by two. This means you are both individuals in an mutually satisfying union.

Your task is simply to know and be attuned to your constantly evolving self so you can listen to yourself even in someone else's company. When you know yourself, it becomes easier to

When the famous writer George Bernard Shaw was interviewed near the end of his life, he was asked who would he have been if he could have been someone else, and he answered, "I would be the man George Bernard Shaw could have been, but never was."

see who others are should their pedestals disappear, especially when you're hot for this guy and overwhelmed with wanting to do and make whatever concessions are necessary for the relationship to work out. It is important to keep yourself and your heart's desires in focus. Knowing who you are will give you the ability to see someone else from a clear perspective.

Earlier we made a Dream list and a Things I Love To Do list to help us become more aware of our passions. Then we made a Daily Routine list to see if what we were doing in daily life was in alignment with our passions. Now we are creating a Lover list so that when we start dating, the people we go out with have more of the traits we want in someone who we plan to take this journey alongside. We will also become better at recognizing the guys that offer what we don't want.

When creating your list, it is of the utmost importance that you are honest with yourself about what you want—namely, someone who supports your dreams and helps propel you along the way. Be who you want to be today. It's really more about you than them. If you are not honest with what you want in a person, and you open your heart to just anyone interested, you may quickly grow tired of dating and overwhelmed by the process. Whatever you want is okay. Creating a

Lover list gives you permission to take credit for what you want and to be proud to stand up for your desires. There is no need to spend a lot of time frustrated with people that can't or won't meet your needs, but this could happen if you're not clear yourself on what those needs are.

Ultimately, you will intuitively know what is important to you. Is it all about money? Then you will need to focus on bringing more money into your life and hang out with other people that highly value money. You may want to go to ritzy clubs, fancy restaurants, or take up a sport like golf. Is it all about religion or spirituality? Then you will want to focus on spiritual pursuits and this may mean frequenting a place of worship or joining a meditation or religion class. Is it all about love? Then focus on loving yourself and doing activities that allow you to give and receive more love. Maybe this means volunteering at a dog shelter, or doing things you love to do. Whatever makes you feel like you are propelling yourself toward more opportunities for love.

Love, Honor, and Trust Yourself First

One of the biggest reasons most people feel dissatisfied or frustrated in their dating lives is because they are approaching dating for the wrong reasons. Perhaps you want a boyfriend because having one makes you feel better about yourself. Or you want to marry a rich guy so that you can be taken care of financially. Possibly, you are afraid to be alone. Or maybe you just want to feel like someone loves you. These are all valid reasons. Problem is, if we seek someone to fix these problems for us, we will ultimately be left wanting more. Entering a relationship out of need will leave us unsatisfied. Our inner needs can only be taken care of from the inside out.

There was a day when relationships were entered more out of need— back when women didn't earn money and men didn't know how to cook and clean and raise kids. Men and women entered marriages almost as a business deal. Each person had a rightful place. Now life is different. We have so many more choices, and domestic roles can be switched around or shared. To enter a relationship for any reason other than to both give and receive love can soon lead to frustration and unmet expectations. That is why it is of the utmost importance to learn to love yourself first, so that by the time someone else comes into the picture, you will be ready for them and not expecting them to be the sole source of your happiness.

Being loving toward yourself begins with being honest with yourself. And this is more than cash-register honesty. It is a level of honesty that will ultimately teach you to love yourself. We suggest that you ask yourself why you want to bring a partner into your life. Are the reasons based in love or fear?

Are you afraid that you will never find someone? That you will never lose weight? Have enough money? Be pretty enough? That you messed up your chances so there is little hope now? Or, do you know that you already have everything you need inside

> *Train yourself to let go of everything you fear to lose. . . . The fear of loss is a path to the Dark Side.*
> —Yoda

yourself right now? We all have a certain level of these fears. The challenge is to discover them within yourself, work through them, and become a loving person that will likely attract someone just as loving.

In life we concentrate on either swimming or staying afloat. When we concentrate on staying afloat, life is all about the struggle. We learn that in order to stay alive, we have to manipulate situations and always be fearful of the impending doom. When we are focused on swimming, we are in the present, not focused fearfully on the future. We know that we are going somewhere and that our own strong body will take us there. We know that the possibilities of where we can go in life are huge and abundant. We are not worried about going under because we know and trust that we can take care of ourselves.

Some Thoughts Before You Start Your Lover List

Rather than concentrating on what color eyes your partner will have, you want to think about the feelings you want them to bring out in you. You want to decide what you want in a person with the wisdom of your heart, not with the excitement of your hormones. You can trust yourself. There is no such thing as a wrong decision; there are only paths of greater learning.

It's a good idea to clarify your intentions in dating first. Ask yourself why you want to date. Do you want a relationship you want to learn and grow from? Do you want to get more comfortable talking to men? Do you want to find someone to sleep with? Do you want to be in a committed, monogamous relationship that is heading toward marriage? There is no wrong intention. If it's your true intention, it is correct. Here are some points to consider:

> *It's not about the exotic trips you'll go on together. It's about who you want to sit next to on the plane for ten hours.*

- **Daily living compatibility.** Are you a morning person? Do you want to date a morning person? Are you the type of morning person that prefers a night person so you can always have quiet mornings to yourself? Are you a nighthawk that likes to go dancing late and sleep in late?

- **Spiritual beliefs and ethics.** How important is it to you that you both share the same religion or beliefs and ethics? For example, if it's super important for you that you marry a Jewish person, you'll think twice about dating someone who's not Jewish. This sounds obvious but for some bizarre reason we go ahead and attach ourselves to someone with whom we'd be setting up problems in the future. We humans are strange that way.

- **Geographic desirability.** One of the benefits to seeing someone is, well, seeing him. This is tough if he lives faraway. But if you're not ready for a full-fledged relationship, having him faraway keeps him from impacting your daily life as much and keeps the relationship from evolving too quickly. We still learn and grow from our experience with him so it's not all bad. Plus, when we do get together it's amazing since we've been deprived for so long. Sometimes we even choose long-distance relationships *subconsciously.* For some reason, deep down only to realize after the fact that we were with him because we weren't ready for the big-time serious stuff with a local beau.

- **Lifestyle compatibility.** What is the dream lifestyle of your lover? Does he travel a lot with work? Is he good with money? Is he a hard worker? A slacker? Does he live life by the seat of his pants?

- **Emotional priorities.** Who comes first? The wife, the kids, work? For our friend Mary, she knew she would come second to the kids with the guy she was with and nothing would come before his career. Being third in line wasn't what she wanted. She knew she had to accept that or move on.

- **What are your deal breakers?** Infidelity, addictions, workaholism, immoral behavior, spirituality (too much, too little) all vary in their levels of importance to different people. The rub here is that the higher charged deal breakers are usually issues we have to deal with in our own lives, so we may attract them to us no matter what. If applicable, we suggest working through some of these issues with a professional so that you won't bring them into a relationship.

Day 21 Exercise: Create a Lover List

We suggest making the list with a friend or two. It helps juice up your imagination. When we did it, we each created our list separately in our comfort stations. These lists started with just a few points, but when we got together, we got other ideas from each other. And we stole from each other. For example, Janice wanted a guy that could hike with her. That made Marni realize she did not want an adrenaline junkie, ten-mile-hike type for a boyfriend. She wanted to be able to go to the gym and go for walks with him.

It is easy to have very high hopes for what we want in a partner, yet be stagnant in stretching our own levels of self-awareness and maturity. After making your list, pick out the top five points. Then promise yourself not to deviate from these points when you meet someone new. If hiking is in your top five, and it is very important to be able to go hiking with your lover, then don't bother falling for someone who loathes hiking. This doesn't make you fussy or high maintenance, it helps you cut to the chase and find someone compatible and appropriate. Also, if these points are truly important to you, then strive to live them in your own life. For example, if adventurousness is important to you in a man, be adventurous in your own life.

> *Know yourself, know what you want, keep the focus on you.*

If you make the list, but don't grow into it yourself, you may have a challenging time sustaining the love that does come into your life. Disappointment is mostly the result of having unmet expectations. That said, a major reason that people don't get their expectations met by others is because they are not up to their expectations themselves. In order to attract and maintain the kind of love you want, you have to first become the kind of person that attracts that kind of love.

Day 22: Beware of Mojo Squashers

See yourself standing up as a mighty force to anything that might try to rob you of your Heart's Desire. Banish from your garden anything that does not encourage growth.
—Sonia Choquette, Your Heart's Desire

While you are happily plotting out your dreams on your Dream list or excitedly describing the lover you're going to meet on your Lover list, you may run across a few Mojo Squashers.

Mojo Squashers don't support your creative dreams and therefore should be avoided at all costs. They don't know that what they say can be hurtful and damaging. They are a danger to your well-being and quite often disguised as friends and even family. They poo-poo your ideas and usually think they are helping you with their opinions, unsolicited advice, and disapproval. Perhaps showing them your dreams brings out an issue or unmet dream in their own life, and they lash out because they don't know how to handle it. Whatever the case, avoid Mojo Squashers or at least step out of their way and let their childish comments bounce off you and stick to them.

> *Don't share your dreams with Mojo Squashers.*

Janice's Mojo-Squashing Friend

I was dating this lovely man. We hadn't really talked about commitments and plans. We were just having fun. Then a Mojo Squasher friend came along, and we had the following conversation:

Mojo Squasher: Have you established that you're officially boyfriend and girlfriend yet?

Janice: Well, no, but we spend all our time together and don't want to date anyone else.

Mojo Squasher: Hmmm. Has he told you he loves you yet?

Janice: Well, no, but I know he does. He shows me all the time. And I haven't said I love him either, but I show him all the time.

Mojo Squasher: Hmmm. What about his income level? Is it in line with what you want in a mate?

Janice: Well, we're just hanging out and having fun. I haven't really thought about it.

Mojo Squasher: "Hmmm. Well, if you want to get married and have a comfortable life, you should really consider these things and not waste time on anyone not in line with your goals.

Then I went home freaking out and thinking we should have had a *commitment* conversation, an *establishing-the-relationship* conversation, a *love* conversation, a *what-about-the-future?* conversation, and a *where-do-we-stand?* conversation?! Then I got really tired and went to bed. Later I realized that all those ideas were in *her* vision, not mine. What was important to me was having fun, learning, and growing. I was learning and growing on my own continuum, learning to trust my own process, and learning to stop doubting myself. So I didn't bother having those conversations with him. But I did stop hanging out with her. She was bad for my mojo.

If there are naysayers in your life who always tell you that you can't do this, or that is impossible, or I wouldn't try that because it's too hard, you want to get away from them. If getting away from them is not possible, start being hyperconscious of what they are telling you and deflect it from you. Hearing someone tell you to be afraid and worried all the time or that your dreams are wrong can be extremely debilitating if you allow it. When we let someone squash our mojo, we're giving away some of our personal power. We're giving away some of our life force. We're saying their life force is more important than our life force so here, take it. We're saying that our pursuit of love is less important than their opinion.

The influence of a Mojo Squasher can block us from tapping into our Creative Vortex and smoosh out all our energy. Then we're left feeling drained and unsatisfied. All relationships involve an energy exchange. We feed and are fed or we feed and we starve. Mojo Squashers are very hungry.

Marni's Dream Home

In kindergarten, I was obsessed with the Berenstain Bears series. They lived in a tree. I wanted to live in a tree, too. I even drew my dream house, which was inside a tree. It had elevators to different branches. My teacher looked at my drawing and said "you can't live in a tree. You can build a house *on* a tree or *around* a tree but not in a tree. Trees are not hollow." I was so bummed that my dream wasn't going to be possible. Then I started to draw tree houses, instead of houses in trees, which is not the same thing. I wish I hadn't believed my teacher and she hadn't taken my drawing so literally. In doing so she became a Mojo Squasher.

> Be who you are and say what you feel because those who mind don't matter and those who matter don't mind.
> —Dr. Seuss

Day 22 Exercise: Write a Note to Your Mojo Squashers

Think back to a Mojo Squasher in your life and write them a letter. No need to send it. In fact, don't send it. Keeps you honest and allows you to be downright cruel if you want to. It can sound something like this: "Dear Scumsucking Tree House Dream Mojo Squasher, no thank you for your reality check. It's not your job. Life is tough enough already."

Repeat with other Mojo Squashers until you feel you've said everything you needed to say to get it out of your system. They don't have to block your mojo anymore. Mojo Squashers can also be people you really enjoy but for whatever reason, throw in a biting comment here and there. Jerks. Feel free to write these messages on big pieces of cardboard in giant letters. Feel free, in fact, to finger paint them. Don't forget which finger to use.

Part 4
Picking Up

Day 23: Fox Hunting and Other Trapping Tactics

Desire, ask, believe, receive.
—Stella Terrill Mann

You cleared your mind in the "Removing Baggage" section, and you learned what you really want in the "Creative Fantasizing" section. Now we're going to learn about getting out there and finding the great love life you want. So where are the great lovers of your future?

Marni's mom is big on dogs. She is always telling Marni to borrow a dog and take it for a walk. She says dogs are great icebreakers. Dog parks are fabulous singles areas. Our friend Aisha met a guy because her dog was playing with his dog. They talked about how they lived close to the dog park. Now they live together.

Soul Mates and How to Find Them

Why is it we are attracted to some people and not others? Did we know them in a past life? Is it as simple as compatible chemicals and energy? Maybe we have lots of soul mates. Maybe we meet them all through our lives to either learn from or lead us to someone else who will be a major influence in our lives. Maybe with some people you can only go so far until you are led to the next teaching by another more strapping individual. If we think about them in this way, then we could be meeting soul mates all the time. No date is a waste.

Six Ways to Attract Soul Mates

1. **Focus on becoming the best you.** You want to be in tip-top condition for the next exciting chapter of your life. This means going for that dream job, taking that class you've been scared to take, keeping your nails trimmed if that's what makes you happy,

and making self-development a priority. Be the version of you that you fantasize yourself to be. Be brave, creative, and sparkly.

2. **Learn to put yourself first.** Whatever you make a priority instead of yourself, you will likely lose. If you put pleasing or being with a man before taking care of yourself, you will end up losing that man. When you respect yourself, he will respect you, or you will find a better guy who will.

3. **Keep yourself fit.** This means physically, emotionally, and spiritually. This also includes drinking enough water, eating nutritious meals, stretching, getting enough sleep, and staying sane.

4. **Don't pretend, lie, or manipulate.** It will always come back to bite your tush. Focus on being honest and kind in all your transactions. It just feels better and helps you sleep at night.

5. **Ask Spirit to bring you soul mates.** And truly believe Spirit will grant you what you need for your greatest good. You will always get what you believe you deserve. Not what you do deserve, but what you truly *believe* you deserve.

6. **Dress slutty.** Also drink a lot and put on lipstick every time you leave the house. Just kidding. Work on developing intimacy with yourself. Not sexual intimacy, per se, but deep self-love. That way you won't *need* to get it from someone else.

And remember, we are all just going through life doing the best we can. All anyone ever does is the best they can. So be gentle and give yourself a break if you slip once in a while.

Where to Meet 'Em

Opportunities to meet people are everywhere. Coffee shops, bookstores, doctors offices, anywhere you see an interesting stranger is an opportunity to strike up conversation. We run around all day doing errands. This is a perfectly acceptable way to efficiently scope for guys. Plus, when you are doing regular things like waiting for your dry cleaning, it's easier to strike up a conversation about what you're doing: "That is a nice shirt you're having dry cleaned." Easy peasy.

Why Bars Can Suck for Meeting Mates

First off, bars are not terrible. There are those "we met in a bar" stories, but they are the exception, not the rule. We've tried (and tried again) to meet guys in bars and have learned something profound: You meet *bar* people in bars. If bar people are your people, then by all means, go out and meet 'em. In our experience, while we had fun (because we always have fun when we're together), the last time we went out to a bar, we met a male porn star, we drank too much, we woke up hung over, and we felt yucky.

The irony is that we go to bars hoping to honestly connect, but what happens is we put on a front the moment we walk in the door. Dressed to the nines, we smile, laugh, try to catch eyes, and appear sexy, intriguing, and fun. We pose while standing confidently in line. We look around constantly, distracted and scoping for someone while all our walls are guarding against unwanted advances. We can't see anyone in this environment for who they really are, we can only see fronts and poses and mostly false advertising. Great way for someone to meet the real you.

> *You're not going to meet someone sitting in your kitchen.*
> —Marni's mom, Sue

Another thing: bars are also very competitive. Everyone is going after the cutest people and the cute people are usually tired of fending off cheesy advances. Everyone wants to leave with someone's number or a promise of nookey. Plus, bars are usually loud and not conducive to conversation. Again, not a great way to meet the real you.

There's more. Don't forget the obvious: everyone is drinking, hence their senses are dull, inhibitions are down, and good judgment is low. In our humble experience, sober mornings following bar nights don't leave us wanting to go back for more of the same. Bars are filled with high expectations and followed mostly by disappointment. Chances are, if you were to see the same cutie from the bar in normal clothes, buying apples at Whole Foods, you'd have a lot better chance at an enlightening conversation. The notion that bars are great places to meet people is a huge myth. The truth is that the best places to meet people is by doing your daily stuff around town. Kill two birds, we say.

There are certain personalities for every singles activity. Find the place where you feel you can shine and act yourself. That is where you want to go. In fact, that is probably where you go already because being there makes you feel good.

Five Obvious Places to Meet Someone

1. **Grocery store.** Hello. Men have to eat every day. Now ask yourself this: Where do they get their food? Do I want a man who shops at a cheap grocery store so we together will one day be eating cheap grocery store food? Or perhaps I would rather have a man who eats at the beautiful, cream-of-the-crop organic, organized grocery store where things are more expensive because they are just better. The kind of guy who doesn't skimp on his stomach and treats his body like a temple. Hmmm. Once you've decided, this is the market you're going to frequent. We prefer a mixture of Trader Joes (all those frozen dinners make it a singles haven) and Whole Foods. We love Whole Foods and could write pages on the many virtues of Whole Foods. Trust us that wherever there is a Whole Foods, there are sexy, healthy singles of all ages. It's the expansive hot food bar that keeps them coming in droves. Here's how it works, if you go:

- **Between 5:30 and 6:30:** The men you will find will be those rushing home to their families or girlfriends. Not always a good time to stroll and scope unless you're looking for a married man, which you are not because you owe it to married women everywhere not to date their husbands—no matter how charming and hot they may be. Even if the husbands tell you they are in a loveless marriage and will soon be getting divorced. Wait for the divorce to be final, but we digress…

- **Between 6:30 and 7:30:** This is when the busy manager types come to do their shopping. They are tired because they are just off work. Observe their groceries to see if they are buying for one or two. Be open to giving your e-mail address or number. These guys could easily fall into the 5:30 to 6:30 range if they had you to come home to.

- **Between 7:30 and 9:00:** This is the single bachelor guy in no particular rush. Great time to find singles, 'cause these guys just came from the gym or their nightly run. Yum. Practice flirting with the person at the deli counter to get you in the flirting mood. Then move over to the hot-food bar. It's called *hot* food for a reason: Hotties eat it!

- **Between 9:00 and 10:30:** Workaholics. They don't have time for anyone but their frozen pizza, a beer, and a bed. These guys value their jobs above all else—often including their girlfriends. Waiting at home so your boyfriend can crash gets old really fast.

Here are some good icebreaker questions to ask at the grocery store:

- How do you cook an artichoke? (You can insert your own clever vegetables.) Have you ever made one before?
- Do you know if this is a good beer? Have you ever tried it?
- Is red wine good with pasta or fish? I have to go to this party and bring wine and I'm the only single girl going.

- If he is near the Ben & Jerry's ice cream . . . Oh my God, have you ever had the Oatmeal Cookie Chunk? It's freaking amazing!
- Is couscous easier to make than rice? Does it take a long time?
- Hey, have you ever had this frozen lasagna? Is it any good?
- How do you make turkey balls? I *love* turkey balls. I could eat them every day.

Make a point of being in line behind Mr. Cutie-with-the-Artichokes at check out. Look in his cart and ask him if his cereal is good. Say anything, just say something. Sometimes the magic word is "Hello." You've got a good three minutes here. Make it count. Today is the day!

Most of our own best meetings have happened when we blurted something out without thinking. In fact, that is how Janice and Marni met each other. Janice opened her trapper without thinking. Men will be flattered and grateful that for once all the pressure isn't on them. It is refreshing. Do you want to spend your time waiting to be approached? Sometimes it seems like we women must love to wait. Just like anything else you want in life, you have to go after love. And do it right away; don't talk yourself out of it.

Over thinking is the enemy. The trick here is not to over think things. If you see someone who catches your fancy, isn't wearing a wedding ring, and is standing alone, just go up to him. Do it before you've had a chance to think. Say hello and tell him you like his watch, then keep talking if he seems interested. If he doesn't, end the conversation and walk away smiling. The trick is to just do it. You must seize the moment. There is no such thing as failure, only people who don't try. There are no rules here.

> ♥ *Smiling and saying hello can be a magical combo.*

It is not like he has to come up to you first, or if you are meant to be together you just will be. Go up and be yourself, already. The point of this exercise is to desensitize your fear of talking to a stranger that catches your fancy. That guy you've seen in the bread aisle that you always notice and get nervous around but never talk to or look at when he's looking will always remain that cute guy you never talk to if you don't talk to him. Rocket science.

2. **Gym.** A lesson to all women: You are allowed to ask questions that you already know the answer to. Men like to help and they especially like help keeping a conversation with the ladies. Though we know a woman needs a man like a fish needs a bicycle, we also know men like to feel like they can offer us the moon. It isn't about 1950s ridiculousness or you being a helpless woman and attracting a big macho know-it-all man. This is about breaking the ice. It's about easy conversation starters that aren't going to leave anyone feeling rejected. So when you're at the gym and want to do weights, feel free to ask for tips from the nearby cute boy. Think of these men like little boys just dying to show you what they've got. It's not too far from the truth.

3. **Bookstore.** Bookstores are great places to meet singles . . . and ones that read, too! Choose a bookstore that has a coffee shop nearby just in case you two want to prolong your mystical meeting by having coffee. Just browse the books and smile at anyone that catches your fancy.

4. **Parties.** Say yes. Again folks, in the spirit of putting deposits into the karma bank, go to parties when you are invited. The beauty of parties is that you and he are usually prequalified because you were both probably invited by the host. It can be super scary to go to parties so some pre–party positive self-talk may be in order. Just tell yourself you're going to this party to have fun because you are a fun person. If you're nervous, you can also say to yourself, "This party will have an awesome and unique essence because I'll be there. They are so lucky." Then walk in with confidence. Body language is a huge nonverbal demonstration of your attitude. Don't walk around with your arms crossed. Stand up straight, smile, and show an interest in other people. Make the party about them and not what people are thinking of you. You'll be just fine.

> *Shyness is no excuse.*
>
> *To paraphrase the great poet Bon Jovi, "It's my life, it's now or never. I ain't gonna live forever." Today can hold seized opportunities or missed ones. Yes, we believe love will happen when we least expect it, but we can't just assume it. Do a little footwork.*

5. **Coffee shop.** Coffee shops are the new bars. They are less noisy and better lit, and you have a higher chance of remembering who you meet. People come for newspaper reading, conversation, and people watching. Coffee shops also encourage repetition. People go to a coffee shop at the same time most days, so if there is someone there you like, you can get to know him over time. Coffee is much cheaper in your kitchen, but who will you meet there?

Marni's Big Epiphany: Cute Guys Are Lazy

Cute guys don't generally ask girls out unless they know they won't get rejected. Marni found this out because she has been an ignorer. While Janice will smile at the guys she likes, Marni likes to ignore them. She had this theory that if she ignored the hot guys that all the other girls are smiling and laughing with, they will be intrigued by her and wonder, "Who's that girl over there and why doesn't she want me, too?" Marni had this fantasy that the hot guy would start to pursue her because she was the one girl who didn't make it easy on him. Hence, he would crave the chase she can provide.

If you are terrified beyond reason to approach someone new, then don't. It can feel scary but it shouldn't feel like you are going to barf. Take baby steps and be gentle with yourself. Aim for something smaller, like eye contact and a smile.

> *Let us reiterate, don't always expect men to initiate contact. That is an old fashioned notion built on social cues that are not always in play anymore. Certain books tell you men are supposed to make the first move. It might be nice, but we disagree. If you don't want to make the first move, at least smile and initiate a light conversation. You don't have to ask him out, but you can give him all sorts of clues to let him know if he asked you out you'd be psyched. You can give him the "come hither" smile, or you can say "hello" or "excuse me." Then see what moves he's got. No need to be too easy.*

So we decided to poll all the cute guys we knew to find out if this theory of Marni's would work. What we discovered was cute guys are lazy. They are far lazier than their not-so-cute counterparts who are asking out most things with a pulse. And just like us, the cute guys also loathe rejection. They are not about to ask you out unless they are darn sure the answer will be yes.

You don't need to be overtly obvious. You don't exactly want to come across as a sure thing. But if you like him, try to let the news get to him. We prefer eye contact and light conversation infused with some innuendos. But you could use the seventh-grade method where you tell one of

> *Our greatest glory is not in never falling but in rising every time we fall.*
> *—Confucius*

your mutual friends you like him and see if the news gets to him. Or inquire about his status with one of his friends who is sure to tell him that you were asking about him. Then again, there is always passing the note that says, "Do you like me? Check yes or no." These are all subtle ways of letting him know you are interested. Appealing to the lazy side but still keeping your dignity. If he disses you after that, it's not like you ever liked him anyway. You just asked a few questions. If he makes a big deal about not being into you, you can say, "Geeze man, don't flatter yourself, I was just curious." Then flee. If the seventh-grade approach isn't appealing, you could revert to our method and let them know you are interested by smiling or striking up an innocent conversation. This makes for little risk of rejection. Most people are glad to have someone talk to them at a party and a little flattery never hurt anyone. Be nice, smile, be friendly and open. How frightening it all seems when we are sober. It's so much easier to talk to a tipsy dude at a bar than a nice guy at the coffee shop. Be brave and open to meeting dates all over town. If there is fear, feel it, let it pass, and do it anyway.

Numbers Game

Some not-so-hot guys seem to play the Numbers Game. They ask everyone out. So when you wonder why only the icky ones ask you out, it's because they are just doing the best they can with what they've got. If you're not into them, just say you have a boyfriend. Janice's imaginary boyfriend's name is Steve. Marni's imaginary boyfriend's name is Gaston.

> *Interesting fact: Fear and excitement produce almost the exact same physiological response in our bodies. The only difference is that when you are in fear you are holding your breath and when you are in excitement you are breathing. To transform fear into excitement, just start breathing.*

Day 23 Exercise A: Talk to Strangers[*]

Not the creepy strangers your mother warned you about, but the cute kind you see in safe places like the gym or the produce section at the grocery store. As the saying goes, do the thing you fear and the death of fear is certain. Start a conversation with a few new people. It can be anyone. Any person can lead you to the person you are destined to meet. The purpose is not to just talk to cute people, but to get used to talking to new people and to feel more yourself when talking to people you are attracted to. Be open to making eye contact, offering a greeting, or smiling at someone you would not usually speak to. Take a moment to allow in their response. If you find yourself embarrassed or feeling weird, notice the discomfort but don't let it stop you.

[*] Part B is coming up in a few pages. Is the suspense killing you? We thought so.

Remember, if you don't do something different, nothing will change. And if someone rejects you, it is not so bad. Your only goal was to speak up.

> *If I had to choose between the girl who's talking to me and the girl who's ignoring me, I'm going to talk to the girl who's talking to me. It's just easier.*
> —Janice's friend Justin

Flirting 101

Flirting is another way to communicate with interesting strangers. It's about looking confident and comfortable. Confidence is the best aphrodisiac. If you're not feeling it, fake confidence as best you can until it comes more naturally. Here are some tips to faking confidence:

- **Stand tall.** Good posture is huge. We need to pull those shoulders back and lift the chin up. Not only does it make us look and feel confident, but it also makes us look *thinner*.

- **Practice a positive internal monologue.** Walking into a party looking hot and telling ourselves that we are fabulous, witty, intelligent, and that everyone here likes us increases our confidence. Why wouldn't everyone like us? We're marvelous!

- **Stay present.** When you're having fun in the moment, you're so much more attractive and people want to hang out with you.

- **Open up your body language.** Crossing your arms and avoiding eye contact sends the message that you don't want to be approached and you're not available. If you don't know what to do with your hands, put one hand in your pocket. Hey, it worked for Alanis Morrisette.

- **Make eye contact.** Keeping eye contact is not only a sexy, flirty thing. It also shows you're confident and sends the message that you are interested in the conversation. But don't stare.

You'll never do a whole lot unless you're brave enough to try.
—Dolly Parton

Day 23 Exercise B: Put Yourself in Front of Him

You see someone attractive from across the room. Go in for the opening line in three steps:

1. Put yourself in front of him. Smile and allow brief eye contact.

2. If you're too nervous to strike up a conversation, don't. Let him. If he doesn't, move on. No biggie. He could have a girlfriend. Whatev. If you strike up a conversation, keep it light and see where it goes. Then see if your first name goes well with his last name. Kidding. Sort of.

3. Repeat with another person.

> *Right now, in this moment, you have everything you need.*
> *—His Holiness, the 14th Dalai Lama*

Notice we didn't force you do anything except walk, which is something you've been doing for years. Luckily, men are really bad at hiding their interest when they find a woman attractive. Pay attention to their body language, and if they are looking at you, smile back. All you have to do is remember the magic word, "Hello," and if he's in, you'll know.

If You're Too Scared

If you'd rather run a marathon barefoot and naked than walk up to someone, yet you feel singlehood is way overrated, know you are not alone. Plenty of people feel the way you do. Even the greatest among us, the ones whose outsides seem perfect, have felt frightened, overwhelmed, deflated, sucky, and small. We hide it as best we can, and soon it passes. So hide your fear knowing you're not alone, take a breath, smile, and walk over anyway.

Day 24: Excuses and Why We Make Them

You don't need a fancy lure when a fish just wants a worm.
—Bob MacLeod, Janice's dad

It is so easy not to get out there, to avoid eye contact, and to live life wearing blinders. We can say we aren't fancy enough, that we don't have the right look, that we are shy and need to lose five pounds first. Basically, we'll say whatever it takes to justify *not* striking up a conversation over kumquats at the grocery store. We can say it's *their* job to initiate everything. All I have to do is stand here and look pretty.

What do we say to that? Excuses, dude. Excuses. If you're going to make excuses at least call a spade a spade. Don't act like it is anything but what it is: an excuse. And an excuse is nothing but fear. And fear only exists up until the point you do what you're afraid of. Once you do it, fear loses its power.

But hey, if your excessive-excuse way works, go for it. However, you're with us right here right now, so we're thinking maybe, just maybe, there is room for movement. So let's ask ourselves why we make excuses for not meeting someone.

One reason may be because we don't really want to meet someone. Seems simple enough, but we may not be getting out there because of something inside us that makes our current lifestyle, whether we like it or not, comfortable and easy and unchallenging. Sure we want to feel loved and have great sex, but all that comes with stepping into the unknown and maybe bringing up issues that need to be healed, so we forget the whole idea. We come up with a bunch of reasons why we shouldn't bother. The reasons are just excuses wearing fancy top hats. We think we're too fat, too skinny, don't have a good enough job, don't make enough money, haven't got our lives together, we're too busy, and so on. Or we make excuses on behalf of the rest of the world. We reason that there are no good men left, men only like skinny girls with big boobs, we're not the right age, work is crazy right now, this town is a hard place to meet someone, and so on.

Often, when we want something that we don't have—a different body, a boyfriend, a better job—we say we want it, but then we don't go for it. We'll stand around being afraid and call it laziness or work or other priorities, but mostly it is just a fear of going for what we really want. Maybe we are scared of being disappointed, or failing, or that we might get everything we think we want and still not be happy. Perhaps we are terrified to get out there and date because we worry about what will happen if we do, and it turns out no one likes us or we are incapable of loving. The big problem with fear is focusing on it. *What we focus on gets bigger, so the more you focus on what you are afraid of, the more you will bring that into your life.* The better thing to do is know that when you are ready, endless possibility awaits.

Common Excuses and Commonsense Solutions

Excuse: I'll be happy when I'm skinny. Make a mini batch of oatmeal cookies! Say your goals are to have fun and learn how to bake but not to gain weight. Well, in Marni's and Janice's case, they have fun baking a whole batch of cookies, then stick most of them in the freezer to eat later in healthy and controlled portions. But then they eat them frozen and eat them all in a short amount of time. Not in line with our weight-management goals, so we cut down a recipe to help us out. How fun to make just enough cookies for you and a friend. And it helps accomplish the goals mentioned above. See the sidebar for a recipe for just two.

Oatmeal Cookies for Two *(cont'd on next page)*

3 tablespoons all-purpose flour
3 tablespoons old-fashioned rolled oats
3 tablespoons sugar
⅛ teaspoon baking soda
⅛ teaspoon salt
Pinch of cinnamon
1½ tablespoons unsalted butter
1¼ teaspoon vanilla extract
1½ tablespoons egg or egg substitute, beaten
3 tablespoons raisins

Place rack in the center of the oven and preheat to 350°. Line a baking sheet with parchment paper.

Combine the flour, oats, sugar, baking soda, salt, and cinnamon. Add the butter and vanilla and blend until moist crumbs form. Add the beaten egg and blend until a stiff dough forms. Add the raisins and mix them in with your hands.

Divide dough in half and place both pieces on the baking sheet. Make sure they are far apart because they will spread as they bake. Bake cookies for about 20 minutes. Cool for 15 minutes.

Yields 2 large and delicious cookies.

Excuse: I'm not sexy enough. It's not about dressing sexy; it's about showing off the best version of yourself. If your intention is to attract the majority of the opposite sex, the majority of men polled say they tend to notice women who dress more feminine. *But,* the widest opinion was that a woman should feel good in what she is wearing. Sexiness shows through your clothes if you're feeling great.

So let the world know you are proud of your womanliness. Sounds obvious but watch any film and you'll see the chicks that look like chicks are the ones the dudes usually dig. And as we all know, movies are just like reality. You don't have to have your boobs hanging out or be all

Our deepest fear is not that we are inadequate. Our deepest fear is that we are powerful beyond measure. It is our light, not our darkness, that most frightens us.

We ask ourselves, who am I to be brilliant, gorgeous, talented and fabulous? Actually, who are you not to be? You are a child of God. Your playing small does not serve the world. There's nothing enlightened about shrinking so that other people won't feel insecure around you.

We are all meant to shine, as children do. We were born to make manifest the glory of God that is within us. It's not just in some of us; it's in everyone. And as we let our own light shine, we unconsciously give other people permission to do the same. As we're liberated from our own fear, our presence automatically liberates others.
—Marianne Willamson

pinked-out and skimpy. And we're not saying if you don't dress like a girl you're not sexy. We're saying that women who look feminine tend to turn more heads. You just have to wear clothes that represent your personal femininity well. For Janice, that means wearing skirts, flip flops, and lipstick. For Marni, that means jeans, Ugg boots, and lip gloss. Generally, having clean hands, fresh clothes, a flattering hairstyle, and a nice scent works well, too.

It's easy to get defensive about dressing more feminine than you usually do because you ultimately want a man to love you for you, not your looks. But how will he love you if he doesn't notice you? To attract his attention, you need to show off your best features. To do that, wear something that helps you feel pretty.

Excuse: I have no time to search for love. One never knows when love will arrive. So when we are running our errands, at work, meeting friends for coffee, catching a matinee, we can be *actively hunting.* That way we don't scare ourselves out of looking for love. While out and about, we want to dress like we are showing off the best versions of ourselves. We don't want to dress like a frump when on the prowl. Wear clothes that you feel comfortable, confident, and sexy in and for goodness sake, stand up straight, throw your shoulders back, and walk like sex on a stick.

If you dress cute, you'll feel cute, and you'll have a better chance of attracting Mr. Cute. We know that feeling confident is an inside job, but when you feel like you look your best, you can feel your best, too.

Excuse: I'm not ready to date. Don't like your clothes? Don't like the way you look? Feel ugly or boring? Then now is the time to take steps toward feeling physically ready. Anyone would be nervous to give a presentation without preparing. Preparation is what helps you feel relaxed and less nervous because

> *I'm not offended by all the dumb blonde jokes because I know I'm not dumb . . . and I also know that I'm not blonde.*
> —Dolly Parton

you know what you're doing. You wouldn't attempt to be the star of a play without learning your lines. If you're not prepared, you have every right to be nervous because you don't know what to expect. You want to prepare so that when you see the cute guy across the room your smile will radiate with confidence.

Excuse: We might not have anything to talk about. Use Marni's interview techniques. In Junior High, I went on a rollerblading date with a guy I really liked. I was nervous and knew I would be the entire night. So nervous, in fact, that I wrote a cheat sheet on the inside of my hand. I wrote things like, "What's you're sister up to? What do you like to do for fun?" I was so nervous during the date that I actually still had to discreetly look at my hand. This method totally worked, and we had a great conversation. Whew!

Excuse: He might get to know the real me and not like me. This is a perfect opportunity to put duct tape over the mouth of your inner critic. Your inner critic wants things to stay the same because the critic can handle only what it knows. The unknown is scary for the inner critic. The best way to ward off this negative self-talk is to turn it around with positive affirmations, even if they feel silly at first. So when your inner critic says he'll probably not like the real you, spin it with, "I am awesome and even if we don't click, I will meet someone else I will click with better anyway."

Excuse: Sometimes I get a little crazy. Life would be lame if every one was perfectly healthy in the head. We would stand around congratulating each other on how perfect we all were. That

The Truth about High Heels

Whether you like them or not, heels make your butt and legs appear more shapely. But oh, the pain! We consulted a runway coach to find out how those girls strut in heels without being in utter agony. It turns out, the way we are used to walking heel-toe-heel-toe in our sneakers is not the way to be smooth in heels. (Why does no one tell us this stuff?) In heels, you are supposed to "step squarely on the balls of your feet. This strengthens the ankles and shifts your center of balance forward, which will keep you from clomping." Also, avoid slouching. Walking with your head held high can make Payless pumps seem like Manolo Blahniks. Well, almost.

We also consulted a podiatrist and self-proclaimed stiletto addict about how long one should honestly expect to be comfortable in heels. Turns out, a woman should be comfortable for at least two hours. You can always get custom insoles or (yikes!) Restylane injections, which last up to six months and allegedly feel like pillows on your feet. Here are three products we like:

1. Cushy pads—for your shoes (footpetals.com)
2. Dr. Scholl's Massaging Gel Ball—for the ball of your foot (drugstore.com)
3. Bliss Softening Sock Salve and Socks—Cool eucalyptus and oatmeal salve and gel-lined socks that soften and soothe (blissworld.com)

may be fine and dandy in Hollywood, but in the real world all that self-congratulatory stuff gets real tired, real fast. Like attracts like. So if you think you're doing fine, you'll attract others who think they are pretty healthy, too. If you want to be with someone who wants you to fix them and bring light to their dreary existence, all you have to do is not work on yourself, focus on the negative, and be motivated by fear. On the other hand, if you want a healthy person in body and mind who is motivated by love and loving, expanding and growing, then keep the focus on yourself, do your own healing work, and you will inevitably attract someone in a similar place. In life you are meant to learn and grow so that you can expand the light of your soul and bring more love to those around you.

Changing Your Attitude Will Change Your Life

The person motivated by fear is apt to bring forth a relationship based on unmet expectations and blame. Marni and Janice know this because we have been this person in the relationship. Frustrated when we don't get what we want and resentful that the other person didn't give it to us and can't read our mind. Or worse, we did ask for it, over and over again, nagging in fact, and still we didn't get our damned needs met. Life became so much better when we shifted our focus to ourselves, concentrated on meeting our own needs, healing, growing, and generally being motivated by love and not fear.

The hard part about changing an attitude that may feel crazy is that it involves just that, change. Change is not always easy because it asks you to examine, adjust, and be really honest with yourself about who you are and what you want. As members of the western world, we seem to always want something for nothing. We want to lose weight without working at it, we want overnight success, and we want love without risking hurt. The thing is, life is not a pain-free endeavor. To be swimming in life, versus staying just above water, one has to know that in order to gain something one has to be willing to let go of something else. (Part of the reasoning behind all that closet cleaning at the beginning of this book.) Change can feel hard because it involves letting go of something that has been a part of our lives for a long time. Even if letting go involves letting go of something that we no longer want—like being alone—it is still a surrender of control and it feels different. While different may not be comfortable at first, in time it can be the catalyst for beautiful change.

No one you meet will ever be perfect. But there is someone perfectly suited to you. With all your imperfections and theirs, the two of you will choose each other to live and grow, heal and expand together. We are all perpetual works in progress. Thank goodness! If we were all perfect life would be boring; there would be nothing to learn and nothing to do.

It is important to know, that like the whole yin and yang thing, life is a cycle of gains and losses. We can't have change without loss, good without risking bad, just as much as up can't exist without down. When we say no to old patterns that we know are wrong even if they feel right, we are allowing space for a new pattern to emerge that we know is right even if it feels awkward. You have to say no to what you don't want in order to say yes to what you do.

Excuses Schmexuses!

Even though we say we want life to be different, the truth is, deep down most of us would rather make excuses to go on as usual, even if it means we are always complaining. We think it is better to make excuses to keep things the same than actually have to feel the necessary pains and losses of life. We would rather make excuses to stay almost comfortable forever than be uncomfortable for a short while undergoing the process of rerouting our life.

> *If you don't tell the truth about yourself, you cannot tell it about other people.*
> —Virginia Woolf

Unfortunately, this is in direct opposition to how life works. Life isn't set up to be too comfortable. We are supposed to be always learning and moving. If we stand still for too long we stop moving forward. When we stop moving forward, we may start being scared and moving backward. Fear fills us up, and we become depressed (we say this from a place of the utmost compassion and personal experience). When filled with fear we are not in the most attractive place to bring in a new love. Frustratingly, this is probably the time when we want love the most. But even then, our head is not in a healthy place and our longing for love is coming out of fear. We hope someone comes along to ignore all our excuses and bring the light back into our gray lives. We want them to fix us but expecting that of someone will ultimately lead to disappointment and blame.

Getting yourself beyond your excuses and into a healthy and loving place is a job for no one to tackle but you. You will start feeling more empowered immediately. It is so empowering to step into the fire we have been afraid of or hiding from, for that is the way to healing and changing the gray into light.

> *The world breaks everyone and afterwards many are stronger at the broken places.*
> —Ernest Hemingway

When we go through these changes, we are removing the walls that may have been blocking our ability to give and receive love. As we remove the walls we create a whole new passage for love.

A Word about What *His* Excuses Really Mean

He's not trying to be a mean guy; he's just sugarcoating how he really feels, which could be confusing. Most guys will do anything to avoid looking like jerks. But if you don't get what they are trying to say then you may force them into being a jerk just so you understand them. Here are some things he might say and their translations.

Excuse: I like you too much to risk ruining the friendship.
Translation: I don't want to be your lover.

Excuse: I'm not ready for a serious relationship.
Translation: I'm seeing other chicks or wish I were seeing other chicks. But if I were into you, I'd be all over you.

Excuse: You would be the perfect girl to marry one day.
Translation: I don't want to marry you today and am buying time until I figure out if I want to marry you at all.

Excuse: I'm not ready for a serious commitment.
Translation: I'm not ready for a serious commitment with you.
(We women must love to wait. We love to wait for a guy who is still deciding if we are worth it. We need to stop waiting. If he doesn't know we are worth it, then he is not worth it.)

Excuse: I promise. (But then I'm going to break my promise or won't make it a priority.)
Translation: I'm okay with disappointing you. (If he doesn't follow through on little promises, he won't follow through on big promises either. An example of a little promise is that he says he'll call on Friday but instead calls on Sunday. Yeah, he called—big deal—but not when he said he would. He shouldn't say things he doesn't mean unless he's okay with disappointing you.) Personally, we like guys who keep their word.

Excuse: I'm confused and unsure about where this relationship is going.
Translation: I'm confused and unsure about where this relationship is going. I don't have my shit together, but I'd be psyched if you wanted to wait around while I get it together.

Excuse: Marriage is a ridiculous institution.
Translation: I don't want to marry you, and I don't want to hurt your feelings. (Is it really about the "ridiculous institution," or is it just about him making excuses to cover the fact that he doesn't see a future with you but wants to keep sleeping with you until he finds the woman he does see a future with?)

Day 24 Excercise: Notice and Take Heed of Your Excuses

Write down any excuses you may have made about the state of your love life. Writing them down will help you become more aware of them as they arise in the future. These self-limiting excuses can then be punched in the nose because they are dumb bullies who are just afraid of change because they don't know what "different" may look like.

A few dumb bully excuses we have made in the past:

- Online dating isn't for me.
- It's hard to meet someone in this town.
- All the good men have been scooped up already.
- Guys my age like younger women.
- I'm too tired.
- I don't have anything to offer.

People who floss on a regular basis have higher life expectancy. Just FYI.

After you've written your excuses, you may notice that excuses are nothing but complaints. Now, stop yourself from saying and thinking negatively for one week starting today. You will be exponentially more effective at life if you start being conscious of negative things you tell yourself on a daily basis. Instead, start spinning any negative thoughts into positive ones. No justifying the negative thoughts, either—"He was wrong! And that's why I'm annoyed." Just spin—"I didn't agree with it, and I feel out of balance. Oh well. I decided to spin it into a positive thing. I'm learning that reacting to his actions in a negative way doesn't serve me. So, I'm choosing to be happy anyway."

Part 5
Dating 101

Day 25: The First Few Dates

*Many go fishing all their lives without
knowing that it is not fish they are after.*
—Henry David Thoreau

Let's get this off our chests first: Dating can truly suck. Dating is like looking for keys you can't find but you know are there. It can feel like a full-time job that you are not getting paid for and like it has a lot to do with luck. So if you are hesitant to date and you don't *feel* like it, you are normal. It is much easier to lie on your couch in your cozy pajamas not doing any work and complain about being single.

First Dates and How to Deal with Them

We may need to go on a lot of first dates before we find a great love. Often we know we're kissing a frog pretty early on, and we scream to ourselves, "I shaved my legs for *this*?!" Sometimes these dates can feel like a big royal waste of time, but we're here to tell you that they are not a waste. It is important to kiss frogs. It is only celebrities that get to rebound right from one seemingly amazing prince to the next. In the real world there is a pretty hardcore law of averages at work. Chances are, the more guys you come in contact with, the higher your odds will be of meeting your great love. The more frogs you meet, the closer you are to the prince. If you have only gone out with two frogs, and you are all discouraged because you think you are never going to find your great love, take comfort in knowing that you just haven't kissed enough frogs to up your odds. Remember, the Beatles had nearly sixty rejections before they were finally signed.

What if they had given up? So itis either that you haven't gotten out there enough, you aren't ready to be dating, or you're going through a breakup, in which case go and read our first book, *The Breakup Repair Kit*. If you are not ready to be dating, you won't see your prince if he dances naked in front of you. Trust that you will recognize him when you are ready. And dates with these frogs may be

---

Definition of the Dating Law of Averages

1) The principle that the more guys you come in contact with, the higher your odds will be of meeting your great love.

2) The principle that over the long haul, things are bound to change sometime.

teaching you the lessons you need so you are ready when your prince comes along. In the meantime, work on making your own life dreamy.

The Test Date

Sometimes you may be on a date and thinking to yourself that you'd rather be at home in bed with your cat. Ask yourself why you'd rather be home. Is it because this guy is boring? Or it is because you thought you were ready to date again but you're really not? Either way it means the date you're on has become a Test Date. These are very important to help you measure your progress. It's okay not to be ready. Thank goodness you went out with him. Now you know. Giving yourself more alone time if you feel you need it is very nurturing and helps get you ready to date again. So for now, ask for the bill, go home, and pet the cat.

The Pity Cup of Coffee

A pity cup of coffee is having coffee with the shy guy that asked you out even though he was scared. You want to give him brownie points for asking you out because you know it wasn't easy. You don't want to hurt his feelings because he is a genuinely sweet guy, but at the same time you know there are no sparks on your part. You say yes because you feel for him, but you don't really want to go. At all. But you've committed to a Test Date to see how you feel about being ready for dating so here you are.

If you said yes, keep your word. Sticking to your word is always good practice. Don't call to cancel. You get to practice being yourself because you definitely don't care what he thinks of you. You practice getting dressed and going out when the stakes aren't so high. You're out and about on a date. Other people see you in the coffee shop looking pretty and having a nice conversation. In fact, this happened to our friend Jane. She was on a crappy date but was being nice about it. Another cute guy saw her. When her date went to the bathroom, he quickly asked her if she and her date were an item. She was delighted to say no! He was super cute. Getting out is important because *you're not going to meet someone in your living room*. If after you've had the pity cup of coffee, the question of another meeting comes up and you really don't want to go for another coffee, here's how to give the heave-ho while smiling and being kind:

1. Start with a compliment from this list to ease the blow.
  a. "I really like this coffee shop. You chose a good place to meet."
  b. "I like your sweater. Looks cozy."
  c. "You sure know a lot about [*insert any topic he went on about*]. I know who to call if I ever need an expert opinion."

2. Use a reason from this list not to continue going for coffee.
  a. "I have had a nice time talking to you, but I'm really not in a place to be dating right now."
  b. "I've really enjoyed talking to you. I have a friend I'd love to set you up with." You get the message to him that it's not you.
  c. If he wants to call you again, say, "Yeah, why don't you e-mail me. Here is my e-mail." He's not worth your cell phone minutes.

3. Then do one of the following activities:
  a. Pick up your keys to go.
  b. Look at your watch and say, "I have to go meet someone now."
  c. Say, "well" the way you do when you're about to get off the phone with a friend.
  d. Stand up and say, "let me walk you to your car/the bus stop/outside…"

Don't ever be too specific about why you don't want to go out with him. No need to over explain. It's gets all weird and awkward. He doesn't need to know, for example, that he is boring and his teeth gross you out. Specifics are unnecessary. Plus, if you don't burn your bridges, he may be more apt to introduce you to his cute roommate.

When Pity Turns to Possibility

Oliver called Marni for a date. "Do you want to go out for coffee sometime?" Marni responded "I don't want a boyfriend and I don't want to have sex with you." True story. This was harsh but she was new at dating and still awkward. Ahem, this was a long, *long* time ago. They ended up going for coffee, which led to dating, which eventually led to sex. They were together for years. Just goes to show that sometimes the people you want to scare away are actually those you're supposed to be with so you can't really screw this up even if you're bad at it.

Marni did not give the "appropriate response." She didn't smile, and she was actually kind of rude. After all, he just said he wanted to get to know her and that he found her interesting. She didn't make it easy on him, and she blurted out whatever came into her head. He still wanted to get to know her, so whatever she said didn't screw things up in the end. Please note: Although we just said you can't screw things up, still focus on being nice. The opposite sex is a lot like us. They get scared and nervous. They worry about stuff, too.

The Top Three Points to Keep in Mind on the First Few Dates

1. **He is your date, not your therapist.** First of all, if you have stuff to work out (most of us do!), talk about it with a therapist or a good friend. Your date should not be privy to the skeletons in your closet until he loves you, or at least has told you he really likes you and even then, he should be told in small doses. The reason is that bringing up these deep issues from your past can bring on a false sense of intimacy and bonding when it is not really there. All you did was show him your dirt.

Don't go on the first date and when he asks if you want a drink immediately go into a litany of how you came to be sober and how AA has changed your life. Just say alcohol doesn't agree with you. Or better yet, say no thanks. If he gets annoyed or pressures you, then you know alcohol is an important aspect of his life, and he may not be for you. Your private life is none of his beeswax yet.

Gift-Giving Karma

Don't start giving your man little gifts in hopes of teaching him that you would like him to give you little thoughtful gifts. It seems logical to give to him so he will get the hint to start bringing you little flowers and necklaces. Rarely do they get the hint. Plus, you give him enough: your friendship, your company, your understanding, your body. A good man will appreciate that and want to give back to you.

You don't need to tell him how your ex-boyfriend cheated on you, that you were bulimic in college, or that your finances are a mess. You don't need to tell him that you hate your mother or that your uncle was sexually inappropriate, and you are dealing with it in therapy. Here is a fresh idea: deal with it in therapy, not with him. If you can't keep these things to yourself because you feel that they are such a big part of you, at least wait until after the first ten or so dates before telling him things that only your good friends know.

2. **He is your date, not your friend.** If this is your first or second date, you should always air on the side of safety. That means that you meet for your date in a public place, you don't let him know your address, and you don't invite him in for coffee. It may seem old fashioned, but you don't know this person. You also want to give him the message that you are respectful of your own safety. If he pressures to drive you somewhere, or wants to pick you up at your house, or wants to go on some hike in the middle of nowhere, or heaven forbid he wants you to come over to his house, just smile and suggest something more public where you can meet, chat, and then go home.

3. **He is your date, not your long-lost friend from fourth grade that's leaving for Nova Scotia tomorrow.** First dates should be a maximum of two hours unless you see a movie and go for coffee, in which case the coffee shouldn't last more than an hour and a half. It's a date, not a marathon. You don't have to fill him in on everything. Let him enjoy your charm and want to hear more from you. Don't hand yourself over on a plate. Let him discover you. If you let him be lazy, he'll be lazy. He won't want more if you keep hanging around. You want to entice him, let him know you're busy living a fun, full life (which you are). If he sees how much fun your life is, he'll want in on the action. Basically, the trick is to suck him in, make him love you, want you, need you, and *then* tell him all your problems (insert sarcasm here). By the time he discovers you're broke, messy, and can't deal, he'll love you anyway. At that time, he'll probably have a few things to share with you, too. No one is perfect. That is what makes love so special—loving each other through our imperfections.

Ignoring Red Flags

A red flag is a warning sign. It either comes from your gut or your head and it causes you to take pause and note what was just said or done. It could be a giant red flag like a wedding ring tan line, or a smaller red flag like him talking about his "psycho" ex-wife. Red flags appear most often in the first few dates, but often we are donning rose-colored glasses so we don't notice. Guys will tell use what went wrong in previous relationships, what problems they have, like whether they have addictions or are prone to infidelity, or even if they aren't interested in a relationship. Believe it or not, most guys are quite frank about their red flags, it's just that we don't want to see them so we rationalize to ourselves that they aren't red flags, or we want to believe we can change them.

Red Flags You May Not Recognize

If anything smells suspect with your new beau, run it by your girlfriends. Sometimes we are so blinded by love that we can't spot red flags. Friends may need to be our voice of reason when we are wearing our rose-colored glasses. A friend of ours was dating this "really amazing, great guy" and was really upset things didn't seem to be working out. None of her friends understood because she kept saying he was really amazing and great. But then she finally told them that they only had sex once every couple of months and it was driving her mad. Her girlfriends informed her that this was indeed a red flag since it bothered her in a big way. It was fine if he didn't want to have sex much; she just needed to decide for herself if it was important enough to end the relationship over and if it was, whether or not she wanted to find someone with whom she was more sexually compatible. Run things by your girlfriends. They'll set you straight.

Rationalizing red flags is an intuitive response. Most of the time we don't even know we are doing it. It is like being in denial. When you are there, it is really hard to step out and see the insanity of what you are doing. A lot of us have denial shrines in our heads that we like to visit, worship at, and sometimes sleep in like a baby. It's very cozy in denial. It usually takes a friend or a lot of honesty on our part to see the forest for the trees. If you like someone, it's easy to only see the good stuff and ignore the bad stuff. Do your best to stay grounded and at least observe the red flags even if you're not ready to do something about them yet. Plus, keep in mind red flags for some may not be red flags for others. For example, if your friend thinks not meeting his family is a red flag but you think it's no big deal, then it's not a red flag for you.

Dating the Same Person Over and Over again

Marni used to go for the needy, lost boys. After much work, Marni realized she was a bit of a control freak and *perhaps* somewhat needy and lost herself. She was so afraid of being swallowed up by a man or a relationship that subconsciously she always picked vulnerable, lost, little boys that were disguised as handsome, masculine men. Some part of her wanted someone with more issues than her so that she could always feel better by comparison and in control of the relationship. Once she began to delve into this in therapy (barrels of fun, by the way) her choices in men began to shift. Thank goodness she didn't marry the cheating alcoholic that always lied to her, though he "loved her," or the floundering artist with a skateboard instead of a car.

> *He who forgets will be destined to remember.*
> *—Eddie Vedder, Pearl Jam*

Now that she is healthier, she is drawn to healthier people that feel more like partners than problems.

Jung knew what he was talking about when he said, "That which we do not bring to consciousness appears in our lives as fate." If you keep bumping up against the same problems over and over, be open to the possibility that this may not be mere coincidence. It's like when you are doing math or an experiment, you always have a constant as a control. While you have different variables you add to the equation, there is one thing you keep constant and unchanging throughout the entire experiment. In your life, the constant is you. The variables are the different people and situations that arise. If you find that you keep coming to the same types of people and challenges, consider that you may be the culprit, not everyone else. At first, such a realization may indeed suck, but in time you will find it makes life exponentially better to find out what you need to work on, or let go of, and then go forth with that knowledge.

> *Be wary of yourself and such magical thinking patterns. They are not based in reality or logic. They are not the truth. Train yourself to recognize your thoughts and disqualify the irrational.*

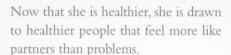

Past Behavior Is a Good Predictor of the Future

If you are thinking someone is going to change from what they were in the past to someone better now that they are with you, be very careful. We women love that fantasy. He loves us so much that he'll change his bad-boy ways for us. We'll turn the drinker sober, the player into a devoted husband. People don't generally change without much work, and even then, their old habits come back occasionally. We want to want someone as is. It is not our job to sign up for changing him.

General rule: If he says he has been a snake, and other people tell you he is a snake, yet you think he doesn't seem like a snake, don't believe that he is not going to be a snake. Unless he is doing or (preferably) has already done the work to change, it is unlikely he'll change because you want him to. Be wary. We are not saying it never works out. We are just saying it is the exception, not the rule.

Warped Thinking

Dating can warp the average person. It can confuse a rocket scientist. It can muddle the mind of a genius. Dating can bring an atheist to her knees. We are such complicated beings. Enigmas actually. Keep this dandy list of ten types of warped thinking handy to remind you of what to avoid the next time you start dating someone new.

Dating Lingo to Avoid For the First Few Dates (and Beyond)

1. **Overgeneralizing.** You see a single negative event as a never ending pattern of defeat and have a tendency to equate one event, time, or person with all subsequent ones. Cue words all, never, always.

   Example: "This has just turned my whole world upside down. I'm ruined."

2. **Disqualifying the positives.** You reject the positive accomplishments or qualities by insisting they don't count for some reason or other.

   Example: "Sure he bought me flowers, but he didn't open the door for me."

3. **Seeing through crap-colored glasses.** You pick out a single negative detail and dwell on it exclusively. Contrary ideas or evidence is ignored.

   Example: "My ass is huge." Despite the fact that your hair is great, you're rich and successful, you're funny, and you're a real catch, you find yourself fishing for insults rather than compliments.

4. **Fortune-telling.** You anticipate that things will turn out badly and feel convinced that your prediction is a fact.

   Example: "I will never love again, and I will die alone."

5. **Labeling and Judging.** Instead of noting a mistake and trying to correct it, you simply criticize yourself with a label. Or when someone else makes a mistake, you attach a negative label to them.

Example: "I can't believe I said something so stupid. What a dork I am." Or, "Hey, look at that loser over there trying to hit on girls. What a tool."

6. **Thinking in Absolutes.** You try to motivate yourself with rigid rules and words such as should or shouldn't, have to, must, or can't. A special case of absolute thinking occurs when you make demands on others, often holding them to expectations that have not been agreed on or discussed.

Example: "If he loved me, he would have moved here for me." We have no idea what goes on in the minds of others, so we can't logically take their actions personally.

7. **Reasoning with Emotions Not Brains.** You assume that your negative emotions/feelings necessarily reflect the way things really are. You feel it, therefore it must be true.

Example: "I *feel* he doesn't really love me for who I am, therefore it must be true."

8. **Blaming Yourself: Woe Is Me.** You see yourself as the cause of some negative external event for which you may not have been responsible. Often a belief in the almost magical powers one has to control events and others. Otherwise known as "It's all about me. Woe is me."

Example: "If I were better in bed, he wouldn't have cheated on me."

Statistic to Smile About

According to the 1995 U.S. Census Bureau, despite the 50 percent divorce rate for first marriages, nearly 90 percent of women will marry at some point in their lives, and most of the remaining 10 percent will either cohabitate or be in same-sex unions. That means if marriage were a deadly disease, you would probably get it unless you were really lucky. Plus, these stats increase for those with a higher education and income level. Statistically, you're doomed. So quit pining. Chances are it is going to happen. Enjoy singlehood while you still can, before the hefty flatulence of your hot spouse and eventual pitter-patter of little feet invades your space.

9. **Catastrophizing.** You exaggerate the importance of things, and you blow them out of proportion. Cue words: terrible, awful, devastating.

   Example: "He's moving away. He's going to find someone better. I'm never going to get married. This is the worst thing in the world."

10. **Thinking in Black and White.** You see things in all-or-nothing categories. Often part of perfectionism, if your performance is less than perfect, you see yourself as a total failure.

    Example: "I'm not good at flirting. I suck and will probably never have a boyfriend."

Day 25 Exercise: Make a List of Your Red Flags

Make a list of all the red-flag qualities and habits your date might have that signal he might not be the person for you. Chances are if you've ignored these red flags in the past, you'll want to ignore them again, thereby repeating patterns. Keep this list and every time you let one pass, put a star next to it. Sometimes things happened five times, and we think they only happened once. Ask yourself if this is the type of person you want to get into a relationship with or if you are just repeating patterns because your subconscious is asking you to learn some lessons already. Here are some personal red flags we have experienced repeatedly. (Not all our red flags will be your red flags, so remember to create your own.)

- He doesn't respect my boundaries. So when I say I want to be in bed by 10:30 and I find that we are still out together at midnight, I feel bad saying I need to go home.

- He doesn't share the need to be responsible with me. I don't always want to be the boss of us. It feels draining.

- He seems too good to be true. He is very charming and seductive and all the girls want him. I have him on a very high gold pedestal.

- He wants a commitment too soon.

- He gropes at me. I'm not into all that PDA all the time.

- He is often late or breaks dates at the last minute. I want someone who respects my time as much as he respects his own.

- He gets jealous easily and lets me know it . . . all the time.

- When we are together it is amazing, but when we are not together he seems indifferent about being with me.

- He is often critical of others, his "crazy" landlord or his "psycho" co-worker. He blames everyone else for his problems.

- He has no problem with me paying for stuff, but he gets cranky when he has to dish out the dough and often seems to "forget" his wallet.

- He has deep anger toward a parent that he obsesses about and doesn't seem to get beyond.

- He doesn't take me to meet his friends or family. He keeps me a separate part of his life.

- I feel like his trophy because he's not nice to me in private, but he's super lovey-dovey when we're out with his friends.

- He has substance-abuse addictions or huge secrets like deep financial debt that I find out about later.

Day 26: How to Have Great Sex

You see, that's your problem. You gotta relax your jaw.
(Don't forget to cup the balls.) Your never gonna win
with those thin bird lips you got there."
—Super Troopers

There is nothing like sex between two people that are mutually hot for each other and in love. If you don't have that yet, the trick is to be comfortable with yourself as a sexual person—knowing what you want and what you don't want, and being able to enjoy your body. Your partner needs to be someone that you feel safe to be yourself with and let go. Then you won't care what your face looks like or if your belly hangs over or if your butt looks big because you will know that you are great and the person you are with is psyched just to be with you. If you trust that the person you are with loves you just the way you are, you will be especially free because you know they will love you all the same after the deed. If you are afraid someone is judging you, you will not only hold back, but you will try to be something you're not. Uninhibited sex is so much more fun. Some say sex is like pizza. Some pizza is so good you remember it forever. But even frozen pizza is never really *that* bad.

How Long Is Long Enough?

Just jumping in the sack before you know someone can give you a false sense of intimacy with someone you may not even like all that much. If you really like the person and think you'd like to try a relationship with him rather than just a sexually satisfying date, then we suggest you wait a while. Wait until you can't wait anymore. Well, if you're supposed to wait until you can't wait anymore, what if you can only wait a week? Is that long enough? Hmm, maybe not so much. We want to force ourselves to spend time in that "nervous, yet not physically connected" phase of the relationship. We want to first connect emotionally and spiritually, so we have a strong foundation for a great sexual life.

The Ninety-Day Suggestion

Oh barf. Are you kidding me? Ninety days is three months. Ninety days is a lot of dates. Ninety days is a ridiculously long time to wait to get laid. I'd go broke just buying batteries if I waited ninety days.

Our ninety-day suggestion may seem harsh, and you may know a happy couple that had a one-night stand and ended up being married for forty years. Do bear in mind that those stories are rare. They are the exception, not the rule. Obviously, if you are just looking to get laid then you don't need to wait, but if you are genuinely looking for a long-standing, loving relationship, then waiting is a good bet. Do note it is our suggestion, not our rule. We're too cool for rules.

Consequently, waiting the ninety days or longer may actually bring you the best lover you have ever had in your life. Let him find out about you and fall in love with you and then you can save the ultimate prize for last. When both of you are willing to wait and get to know each other like this, a few months after you do finally start having sex you will be very uninhibited and free. Plus, you're more likely to hang out together outside of home a lot more because if you're home all the time, you'll want to make out and if you make out, you'll want to hit it already. Not to mention that love and respect for each other will be involved, and sex will be a deeper experience for the both of you. Make sure both of you are cool with waiting.

This is a huge way for you to show him that you respect yourself, and he will respect you, too. If he pouts or he won't stick around for that long, then you know this wouldn't have lasted anyway and, in that case, is he really worth sharing yourself with? Remember, never chase. That's not your job. Your job is to be the best version of you. Besides, there are plenty more where he came from. Just go to the grocery store or coffee shop.

A lot of women today don't seem to be choosy enough. Let us remind you that biologically women are supposed to be choosy. Biologically, it works better for us to only accept the choicest men that have proven their sperm is worthy of our egg. Men on the other hand have a boundless amount of healthy sperm always ready and raring to go. Biologically, they are programmed to want to spread their seed across the land. We have the great fortune to be programmed to be choosy.

> *Never chase after a man or a bus, there will always be another.*
> *—Marni's mom, Sue*

Besides protecting you both physically and mentally from a lot of negative stuff you don't need, waiting will keep your minds clear. When we jump into a sexual relationship too soon, we immediately establish a false sense of bonding. You suddenly feel that you don't want to lose this person that you essentially don't even know. This may make you feel clingy and unattractive or even disgusted. Just the opposite of what you wanted.

Also, when we start to fall in love, especially if we are sexual right off the bat, our hormones will make us cover up red flags. Guys will show you who they are within the first month. Your challenge is to see it and believe it. In all the couples we surveyed, most doubts that were felt on the first date were still there years into the relationship.

Three Ways We Fall for People:

1. **Falling in lust.** Relationships that have a strong foundation of physical intimacy. When the physical dies down or gets comfortable, we begin to wonder why we are with this person. Brunch gets boring, we start to miss hanging with our friends, and we wonder when he'll go home already.

2. **Falling in lost.** Relationships that have a strong foundation of needing to soothe the self and avoid being alone. They have very little to do with the other person, and are based on what you want for yourself right now to make you feel better. Artists *love* to fall in lost. They dig the torture, the drama, the tears, bla diddley bla.

3. **Falling in love.** Relationships that have a strong foundation of goodness and spirituality. You truly want what is best for yourself and for the other person, even if that means understanding that true happiness for the other person may trump staying together.

Equality: Knowing Your Worth

You're just as great as he is, and he's just as awesome as you are. Together you are a force to be reckoned with. Feeling like an equal partner in a relationship keeps the sex hot. When two people feel free to be open and expressive by day, they both feel passionate, free, and uninhibited by night.

Equality is about knowing that both of you are on the same level. Neither of you feels like you are better than the other. Both of you feel lucky to be with each other. It is about not being afraid to speak up about something that is bothering you. Often times, one partner may be afraid to bring up an issue because they don't want to upset the relationship. Then they stew, and the other person doesn't understand what's happening; they only know what's *not* happening between the sheets.

When one partner doesn't feel as worthy as the other, they may be afraid of upsetting the balance and being dumped. This doesn't make for a good sex life, which in turn doesn't make for a good relationship. The two of you want to know the relationship feels good for both of you. You don't need to be equal in status, looks, or finances. Nor do you need to be of the same religion or ethnicity. But you do want to view each other as equals in values, spiritual paths, and future plans. You do want to respect each other and be willing to grow and face life together. Studies on relationships that work show that both partners think of themselves as a "we" when facing life's big decisions. What will *we* do? How will *we* handle this? Will *we* move for your job? When you both think in terms of what is best for the relationship during the day, you tend to think of what's best for both of you at night.

If you're not making decisions equally, one of you is giving away your power to the other. The two of you must feel like you contribute equally to the relationship. If one person feels less important, they may start to feel fearful in the relationship. They may start to hold back their thoughts and try to please their partner rather than be authentic. They may also start to resent their partner. When you're equal, you'll both feel you're in the boat rowing together, and neither of you will be afraid the other will jump out. Knowing you're both in the boat will bring confidence to your relationship.

Marni and Bill had an unequal relationship. Bill wasn't contributing as much to the relationship because he was hot and rich and felt Marni was lucky to be with him. He loved her but felt superior to her because he thought he was a better catch. Marni didn't feel confident about herself and started to be careful about what she said around him. She would try not to upset him and would censor herself fearing that if she voiced certain fears, he would leave her.

Soon she started to feel resentful and irritated with him because she was stuffing so much of her feelings down. For example, when he left the bed unmade even after she asked him to make it when he was the last out of bed, she would feel far more rage than was appropriate for the situation. Small irritating things he did started to magnify into huge annoyances. As these annoyances built up, she would simultaneously censor herself because she felt that if she told him how she felt, he might leave her.

At the same time, Bill was not being forced to grow and improve himself because his partner was afraid to challenge him. This was frustrating and spiritually stifling for both of them. Bill's passive way of dealing with this frustration was to unconsciously do things that would annoy her like "forgetting" to make the

> *You've got to learn to live with what you cannot rise above.*
> *—Bruce Springsteen*

bed, flirting with other women, or leaving a mess. Eventually this stress was reflected in their sex life. When they brought all their negative feelings to bed, the passion was gone.

Feeling Needy and Hating It

Neediness is an interesting concept. The biggest reason we don't like when other people are too needy is that it triggers our own fear of being needy. Many of our clients come to us complaining of their own neediness and how much they want to get rid of the feeling. Male clients feel that it makes them lose self-respect; female clients feel that it turns them into nags. In either case, it affects performance in the sack.

The truth, which feels unfortunate to some, is that we human beings do need each other. We continuously need to work on taking care of ourselves and to allow ourselves to guiltlessly receive care from others. While the traditional family structure may be different nowadays in that

> *Don't nag. It doesn't work anyway. You can ask for what you want once. Maybe twice just to "make sure," but more than that and it's nagging. If he doesn't comply, accept it or move on. You are accumulating good information about the kind of person he is. Do you want someone that doesn't listen to you or lies to you? Yeah, we didn't think so.*

women no longer need a partner for financial stability, we still need love and support. It would be a lonely life if we didn't. If you feel needy, don't berate yourself. You are human and lovely.

Neediness has become such an ugly concept in society that many of us, especially women, have forsaken the idea that they should be treated with a certain amount of value and respect. In order to not appear "too needy" or "too naggy," some end up unhappy because they are holding back so many needs. It is hardly "too naggy" or "too demanding" to enter into a relationship with someone and expect that you will feel loved, valued, and respected.

That said though, if you are not able to value, respect, and love yourself, it is insane to expect someone else to do it for you. Self-love is an inside job. Someone else making you feel loved will not sustain you for long. However, you are entitled to feel that you are valued and respected by the person you are with. Needing others, wanting to deeply connect, love, and be loved is part of what it is to be human. Love involves a certain amount of surrender and vulnerability, and hence, if you want to call it so, neediness.

Marni's Account of Feeling Needy

For a long time, I felt like I only attracted needy men, and after awhile it started to disgust me. Then I fell head over heels in love like I never had before. All of a sudden, I started feeling needy and I *hated* it. It felt icky to me to feel I needed such consistent reassurance that this man loved me. This feeling went on for awhile until I realized two things: one, that I needed to do some more self-work to love myself better, and two, that my neediness was actually well-founded. Though I can always use more self-work, upon closer inspection in this particular case, I was also dating someone who was rather unavailable. I was feeling vulnerable, as falling in love should feel, and I was also feeling that my needs were not being taken into much consideration. Some of the things that I felt naggy about or too demanding to ask for were things that any person with a healthy amount of self-esteem should be asking for. I held back, and it ultimately taught me the lesson that I deserved more.

Celestial Connections: Sex by the Stars, the Sun, and the Moon (Courtesy of astrologist Brenda Knight)

The best relationships happen when one person's moon sign is the same as the other's moon. Opposites also attract as many a lusty Leo and quirky Aquarian can attest, so you should also check out the person right across from you in the zodiac. Some of the most delightful and exciting sex can happen when people are very different and compliment each other with refreshing new sex techniques. This book is not big enough to contain all the necessary star charts, so I recommend a resource like *www.astro.com* for excellent *free* charts, daily horoscopes, and much more. Here are the basics concerning sun signs. Please bear in mind that these astrological signs can vary a day or so from year to year, so you really have to consult a professional.

Fire Lovers

Fire signs are intense, usually positive, and often impetuous. They get things moving. They are passionate and need an enthusiastic match in the bedroom. Fire signs belong together. Sparks can also fly if your Moon or Venus is in a fire sign.

- Warrior **Aries** angers easily, but the "kiss and make up" part can be fun.

- Tell a **Leo** they are wonderful and sexy (and they really are), and you will be amply rewarded with dramatic fireworks between the sheets.

- Adventurous **Sagittarius** likes to make love outdoors. I recommend a hike followed by skinny-dipping and an erotic "workout."

Air Lovers

Air signs are the great communicators and philosopher-techies of the zodiac. They are always thinking. These fun and social creatures really get along with everyone, although earth signs may try to keep them too grounded. They live in the world of ideas and can sometimes intellectualize sex. You can turn this trio on with sex toys and books of erotica.

- **Geminis** are very verbal during sex, so a little erotic talk can drive them crazy with desire!

- **Libras** are the most partnership-oriented of all signs, so a very romantic approach will bode extremely well here. Libras are ruled by Venus and have refined lovemaking to an art form.

- **Aquarians** are wildly experimental. Together, you'll go through all the *Kama Sutra* positions and beyond.

Earth Lovers

Earth signs are at once solid and practical and extremely sensual. Grounded and security-oriented, they are the most involved with the physical body of any sign in the zodiac.

- **Taurians** are ruled by Venus, so they are very amorous. Bring a fine wine and some food into the bedroom for an after-sex snack. Soft fabric, good music, perfumed oils—all senses are explored with Taurus bulls in bed.

- **Virgos** are not fussy neatniks; they are highly skilled lovers. I should know since I married one! Virgos are service-oriented—a wonderful attribute, erotically speaking.

- **Capricorns** work just as hard in the bedroom as they do in the boardroom. Support them as they strive for success and you will be amply rewarded by an attentive lover who will sweep you off for weekend trysts.

Water Lovers

Water signs are the most emotional and sensitive of the zodiac. These people feel things intensely, and their empathy and sensitivity can make for exquisite sex. A passionate group, to say the least.

- **Cancers** are very nurturing. This is a lover that will take care of you and meet your every need, sexual and otherwise. They are home-oriented, so the bedroom should be a palace with every comfort and erotic toy.

- **Scorpios** are reputedly the most passionate of *any* sign—they are walking sex and they know it! They love mystery and want to make love for hours on end. In bed and out, they want to dominate and own you. Whisper in their ear that you want that, too, at exactly the right moment for ultimate pleasure.

- **Pisceans** are dream lovers and so intuitive they can anticipate your every need and give you unceasing sensuous attention. These trysting fish would *never* get out of bed if they didn't have to!

Day 26 Exercise: One Consenting Adult

This is definitely one of the most fun exercises in the book. Tonight you're going to pleasure yourself. That's right. And you're going to rock your world like no one else has! Let your mind wander. You even have our permission to think about people you probably would never do in real life: the unsuspecting delivery guy who drops off a "package," or the room service boy who delivers more than just your meal, or the taxi cab driver who . . . oh, you get it. The mind is the most powerful sex organ after all. If you aren't in the practice of such things and have a few inhibitions, we suggest some toys. Booty Parlor is an online store where you can find tasteful and effective toys to assist you with this exercise. Their address is *www.bootyparlor.com*. The best part is that everything is delivered by a delivery person who has no clue what you've ordered. Imagine that!

> *I think everybody knows
> what we need to do.*
> —George W. Bush

Day 27: How to Ruin a Relationship

How are you? Miserable as usual. Perfectly wretched!
Where are they? For heaven sakes, where are they?
—Cruella DeVille

Veronica Kaplan was desperate to have a boyfriend. She thought having a boyfriend would fix her and make her life full. She went out on countless dates, dated a few of them for a month or so at a time, and still they were dropping like flies. Veronica was cute! She was super friendly, smart, interesting, had a great career—all that good stuff. Yet really cool men continued to opt out after about two months. Let's learn from her so we can bypass the nonsense. Here's a few things she did wrong:

- When a guy showed interest, she dug her nails in.
- She called him incessantly to chat. When he wasn't at home, she would call his cell phone, then when he didn't answer right then, the first thing she would say when they did talk was, "Why didn't you answer your cell phone?" or, "Where were you earlier?"
- She was the predator, not the prey. If you want to be treated like prey, you can't act like the predator. Prey get wooed: predators do work.
- She was always initiating the date. Not that this is always bad, but let him ask at least half the time.

- She insisted on going dutch on a date because she thought it made her more appealing to him. It didn't. A lot of guys wanted to make her feel special by paying but she wouldn't let it happen. She came off as cold and closed.
- She went toward dating with a sense of scarcity, not abundance, i.e. she was afraid of losing him, so she never backed off.
- During a phone call, she talked and talked and talked even after he said he should go.
- She completely ignored red flags. When he didn't get her anything special for her birthday, she convinced herself she wasn't bothered by it even though she was.
- She told all her friends everything about the relationship, so they knew more about what was wrong in their relationship than he did. She even forwarded his e-mails to her friends, knowing he would be horrified if he ever found out.
- She didn't give him freedom to be the man. She wanted to rule the relationship. She wanted to control everything under the guise of making things easy for him. The result was that she wasn't giving him the opportunity to surprise her and shower her with love. She was holding him too tightly.
- She complained to her friends behind his back about the "measly" gifts he bought her.
- When the relationship went sour, she would make racist remarks about him.

- She never took responsibility for what was wrong in the relationship. It was always his fault. He was never good enough.

And that's not all . . .

Veronica Acted Like His Mother

Take out the "s" and the word "smothering" becomes "mothering." This isn't coincidental. If we don't want to set up that sort of relationship then we don't mother him. Period. He may act like a baby and seem to need mothering at times, but if we get in the habit of doing it all the time, we set ourselves up for failure. Instead, if we let him have his life while we have ours, then we won't feel taken for granted. In fact, most mothers do feel taken for granted by their children at times. You are his lover, not his mother. If you want to feel especially nurturing, start gardening or obsess over your pet. There are more fun ways to keep your man satisfied than being his mother. Let his mother be his mother; you be a mother to real children instead. And bear in mind, most men are raised to *eventually* leave their mothers for another woman.

Veronica Wrongly Analyzed His Lack of Interest

"It was so good at the beginning. Later, things were still good . . . when we were together. But weren't together much near the end. He was busy with work." Suspect. In fact, he didn't call her for plans every weekend or most nights before bed. We want to believe that things haven't changed, but something is off. His actions seem different, and we think maybe he's just comfortable. Maybe he's just busy at work. Maybe he misses his friends. Maybe Veronica started to feel a little less important because of how she clung to him; he may have turned away just to get some time to himself.

Men are not as complicated as we think they are. Instead of trying to figure him out with her girlfriends, Veronica should have taken the hint: He didn't hang out with her because it was not his priority to hang out with her. It was tough for her to accept that her guy had lost interest because she remembered how good it used to be and how good it felt when he was into her. Problem was, those moments that he was into her became fewer and farther between. If she felt under appreciated by him, chances are she was under appreciated. Other things were taking priority because he thought he already had her in the bag or he simply lost interest. This was a good point for Veronica to be honest with herself and get out before the ship sank.

When He's Interested, You'll Know

No need to spend time trying to figure out why you've been hanging out so long and he still hasn't asked you out, or why he only asks you out every three weeks, or why he doesn't call you as much as he says he thinks about you. This is why:

He's not interested enough. Period.

He may in fact think you're cute, may have enjoyed sleeping with you, may even think you're the perfect girl to marry one day, but it's all bunk. If you were the one for him, he wouldn't be leaving you open to be snatched up by another guy. He would want to ensure he's the only guy snatching you up.

Okay, we're sounding bitter. We really aren't. We like guys. A lot. We have a great fondness for a few in particular. Our basic message is this: Date guys that show you they are interested in you, so you don't have to question whether they are. They will step up and be the best boyfriend they can be for you if they like you enough. No need to settle for less.

That old saying "Actions speak louder than words" applies to guys. They speak loudest through their actions. They may say they are all into you, but you must read their actions to get a true sense of how they feel. Also, listen to their words. Often men will tell you exactly what they are thinking but they will disguise it with an "I really like you but I'm screwed up" tone. They also may not be able to *say* how they feel, but they show you by giving of their time and energy.

Languages of Love

Be open to the different dialects of the language of love. Some men's language of love is different from others. He may not tell you he loves you every day, but he will wash the dishes every day and fix your garbage disposal when it makes that gurgle sound. This may be his language of love: showing through doing.

Janice's Story: The Man Who Showed Me but Didn't Tell Me

So I'm dating this guy and we got to a point where it seemed about the right time to ask where this was going. He got all quiet and weird. He pondered for awhile and said he didn't know and didn't understand why we had to define anything anyway. Then a week went by and he broke it off. See, he didn't want to be a boyfriend because it meant a whole slew of things he wasn't ready for. Though it pained me, I had to accept this and let it go. This sucked big time. Oh the torture, the suffering, the sleeplessness. But what was I to do? Say that was fine? It wasn't fine. Then he started inventing very important reasons to see me. It was all very cute and transparent. Eventually he just kept showing up, kept treating me kindly, and kept wanting a deeper connection. See, I wanted him to *tell* me, while he wanted to *show* me. There are many languages of love. Him showing me was pretty great.

> Don't put your life on hold to wait for him. It's not a trial run. This is it, your whole life. You don't get to do it again.
> —Marni's dad, Bernie

Marni's Story: The Man Who Told Me but Didn't Show Me

I went out with a guy for over four years. In the first week he told me of his past problems with infidelity. However, he softened this truth by being honest and telling me it was something he wanted

> *Honor him as he is because we are all constantly changing.*

to change. Being the helpful camper I am, I fell in love with his honesty and desire to work on himself. I ignored that usually someone's past will predict their present and future. I decided to trust him, figuring if he told me about his problem with infidelity, he was probably over it. Besides, who would cheat on fabulous moi? I'm special. I'm different from the other girls. Fabulous, really. Well, I wasn't; at least not to him. He cheated on me like he did with all the others. I spent four years to find out a truth he had already told me in our first week. Take note: Men will tell you who they are through their actions or their words. You have to be willing to watch or listen to find out the truth.

And then there are those who tell you but don't confirm their words with their actions. Here are some examples:

- He says he wants to get to know you better but then he takes you to loud bars and other places not conducive to chatting and getting to know each other better.

- He says he's in love with you but then he cheats on you.

- He says he wants to spend time with you but he's either too busy or the time he spends with you isn't quality time.

- He says he's totally hot for you but doesn't want to hold your hand.

- He says he wants to marry you but doesn't ask you to marry him . . . ever.

- If he's not calling you, you're not on his mind. (Don't call him and ask if he's been thinking about you. That's fishing.)

Back to Veronica . . .

Veronica Didn't Stand Up for Herself

Veronica asked Ivan to get an AIDS test. He agreed, but then never had time, or didn't know where to go, or went and it was closed. These excuses helped him put it off without having to take responsibility. This went on for months. This issue caused much fighting and resentment between them. Every time they made love, Veronica was anxious and worried and wished he would get tested already. Sure, she could have withheld sex until he got tested, but she didn't want to have to be in the position of "punishing" him when he misbehaved. Not to mention they had great sex. Ivan's actions told her he didn't care enough to put her mind at ease. If a guy is not making simple efforts to put your mind at ease and you find yourself in a reoccurring fight, consider that he doesn't respect your feelings or needs and this may flow into other aspects of your relationship. Not cool. You can do better.

Veronica Didn't Take the Hint

"I kept asking him where the relationship was going. But I cut it down to only once a day. I wanted to know." We are allowed to initiate this discussion on one condition: we initiate it once, we listen to what he says, and if we don't get the answers we want, we move on. You don't get to initiate this discussion every two months hoping his answers will change. Don't think you can change him, even if he says he's trying to change. He may be trying really hard, too. How very touching, but he is also buying time. *Your time.* Don't spend time with a guy that makes you wonder how he feels about you. Repeatedly asking him makes us look naggy. If he's still not giving the answers we want or showing us in a loving way, then we need to accept this or move on. Remember, guys that are into you will want to be your boyfriend because they will want to ensure no one else snatches you up.

Veronica Loves Who He Might Become Instead of Who He Is Right Now

Veronica tried to mold her man into what she wanted. Or she tried to make him who she thought he was when she started dating him. She would have learned more about life by doing her best to love someone as is. Again, no one is perfect. Even someone who seems perfect at first, isn't. People will continually disappoint her if she expects them either not to change or to change into something she deems better. Rich guys can go bankrupt, perfect abs can turn into a beer belly, sex drives can increase or decrease, hairlines can recede. Life is about letting go and accepting. Enjoy what is now and let go of what isn't.

Day 27 Exercise: Are You a Veronica Kaplan?

Take this quiz to find out.

1. What do you do when he has a headache?
   a. Turn the house upside down to find him an Aspirin.
   b. Get a headache in solidarity.
   c. Feel sympathetic but continue doing whatever you were doing.

2. What do you do when he unfairly loses his job?
   a. Constantly search the Classifieds circling ads to give him later.
   b. Call his old boss and start bitching him out, then start telling everyone about the unfairness of how your boyfriend lost his job. In fact, it's all you can talk about.
   c. Feel sad for him but offer him encouragement and remind him you'll be a supportive friend and lover through this time.

3. What do you do when talking to your friends?
   a. Always bring up a story about him more often than you do about yourself.
   b. Friends? You don't have time for friends. You have a boyfriend.
   c. Nothing much has changed with my friends. We still hang out, talk, and have fun.

4. It is a friend's birthday Saturday and at the last minute his work is cancelled so he invites you on a romantic weekend getaway. What do you do?
   a. Don't go to your friend's birthday and call the next day to tell her how ill you were the night before.
   b. Decide you'd much rather go rendezvous with him, so you call your friend to apologize for not being able to come to her party.
   c. Tell him you are so excited to go away with him but it will have to be after the party or on a different weekend.

5. You're shopping with a friend for the afternoon and your boyfriend calls. You had planned to meet him at 8:00 p.m., but it's 3:00 p.m. now and he says he's free and wants to hang out. What do you do?
   a. Leave your friend to go out with him. You were only killing time with her until he was free anyway.
   b. Keep hanging out with her, although you secretly want to dash to his house. You think of him all afternoon and buy him a present.
   c. Tell him you already have plans with a friend, and you'll see him later.

Scoring

Mostly A's: Consider that you may be strongly attached. This indicates that you would be willing to put your own life on hold for his life. The foundation for a strong, loving, and equal relationship involves remaining an individual and staying true to yourself even if it feels better and easier to be with him. Be wary that being too attached can be a strong sign of codependence and addictive-relationship behavior. We're not saying this is bad behavior. We just want you to be conscious of what you're doing. Awareness is the first step toward change. When you put him before you, you end up losing you—and sooner or later, the relationship, too. Remember, it's like they say on an airplane: Put the mask on yourself first.

Mostly B's: You're on the verge of jumping out of your life and straight into his. You know where your boundaries are but you're flirting with codependency. It is completely normal in a relationship to waver between different degrees of codependency and individuality. But remember, if you put him before yourself, your relationship will usually sour.

Mostly C's: You're an individual woman with a strong sense of self. Not only are you happily living your own life, but you're making your relationship stronger. Satisfying relationships are the combination of two whole people. Nice job.

Ten Signs of Attachment

If you scored mostly A's or B's, read this!

1. You put your opinions, beliefs, and preferences second to his.
2. You often change your behavior to please him.
3. You worry about what he is thinking about you . . . a lot.
4. You worry about what he is thinking about everything.
5. Your mood is strongly affected by his issues, anxieties, and worries.
6. You stay in a relationship because you're afraid of being alone.
7. You're dependant on him in some way—financially, emotionally, or for status.
8. You fear if he left, you would be a lesser person.
9. You don't worry about things that are or aren't going on in your life, only his.
10. You measure your self-worth by external things like how much money and status you have, how you look, the kind of car you drive, and how much people like you.

Answering yes to even one of these may be a strong sign of attachment. Just be more aware. Awareness is the easiest way to shift perspective. You are already steps ahead just in reading this book and doing the exercises. Bravo!

You are attached if another's life becomes more about you than it is about him or her.
—Stephen C. Paul

Day 28: How to Be Happy in a Relationship

Don't rely on someone else for the happiness you can give yourself.
—Iyanla Vanzant, author

The secret to being happy together is being happy alone. When we seek someone out because we feel lonely and don't make ourselves happy, we are seeking someone to do a chore for us that is not their job to do. When we expect such a powerful result from someone, we may ultimately be disappointed. No one can fill you up and make you happy if you don't know how to do it for yourself. Aye, there's the rub. It's like filling up a container with a small hole in the bottom. But if we enter into a relationship already knowing how to make ourselves happy while enjoying someone else's company, then we can love them without expecting anything in return. We will be happy rather than disappointed.

When we fall for someone else because they make us feel happy inside in a way that we don't know how to make ourselves feel on our own, we risk becoming emotionally dependent on them for our happiness. We begin to need them like a drug, as all the romantic movies and songs talk about, and someday we may feel like we are nothing without them.

> *I do actually believe in love. I can't say that I'm 100 percent successful in that department, but I think it's one of the few worthwhile human experiences. It's cooler than anything I can think of right now.*
> —Trent Reznor, Nine Inch Nails

Why would we give our partner all the responsibility for making us happy? Why would we give them the job of boosting our self-esteem? Ultimately, if a partner does a good job of making us feel beautiful and funny and generally good about ourselves, then we start to call that being "in love." But really all we have done is attach ourselves to each other and created the expectation of needing them to fill us up. We have not created love, we have created emotional dependency. The difference may seem slight but it's huge. Emotional dependency is different from love because it is born out of fear. We all experience emptiness inside and when we expect it to be filled by someone else, we deprive ourselves of our own capabilities. We can gain the most happiness by learning how to build our self-esteem and telling ourselves we are beautiful and funny and terrific instead of depending on someone else to do it for us.

> *This is the miracle that happens every time to those who really love: the more they give, the more they possess.*
> —Rainer Maria Rilke, poet

When we enter into a relationship with someone because we like them and they like us, but we do not expect to fill each other up, we are each free to grow and be happy together without

> *To love means you also trust.*
> —Joan Baez

resentments or expectations. Think of a relationship as if it were a dance. When we are young, we think the best relationship looks like two people dancing close with their bodies stuck together. As we mature, we learn that the most successful dance is two people twirling around each other. They each have their own space but also want to be in each other's company.

He Says He *Wants* the Job of Filling You Up

The problem with someone else wanting to fill you up is that he may not know what he is signing up for. He may hope to fill you up on the condition that you fill him up in other ways. Ultimately, you may both find yourselves frustrated and unhappy and wondering where

*Things that **won't** fill you up in the long run:*

- ♥ Someone else
- ♥ Sex
- ♥ Drugs
- ♥ Food
- ♥ Alcohol
- ♥ Money

*Things that **will** fill you up in the long run:*

- ♥ You
- ♥ Self-love
- ♥ Spirit, spiritual exercizes
- ♥ Meditation
- ♥ Following your dreams
- ♥ Service to others
- ♥ Forgiveness

you went wrong. You may blame each other for not being the kind of partner you both thought you wanted, because what you really wanted was someone to do the inside job that you are both supposed to take responsibility for yourselves. But then, it is much easier to blame someone else than to learn how to fix yourself. Movies and romantic songs don't help. They constantly send messages about how we are to look for someone else to make us feel good about ourselves, or if it's a breakup song, it's about how the other person ruined everything.

Like Attracts Like

We can't have a healthy relationship until we ourselves are healthy. The real danger in looking for someone else to make us happy is that instead of finding someone who is truly happy himself, we will find someone just like us—someone looking to be made happier. Like attracts like. We may not even realize it, but if we are looking for someone to fill us up, we will attract someone who also wants to be filled up. That's great at first, and then it will inevitably get messy because neither of us will be getting our needs met, and since we don't know how to meet them ourselves, we will continue to seek out inappropriate people and hope that they will meet our needs. In the end, we both end up feeling empty at some point because that is how we entered the relationship. Two empty people cannot fill each other up. Ultimately, no one can give us something we don't have or can't give ourselves.

> *When human relationships fail, they fail because they were entered into for the wrong reason.*
> —Neale Donald Walsch

On the other hand, if we learn how to fill ourselves up and start dating knowing our own worth and how to make ourselves feel lovely and beautiful and special, we will already be filled up and won't come at people from a place of neediness. Healthy people that are also already overflowing with love will flock to us because they will want to share what they have. Again, like attracts like.

Neither person will be dependent or scared of the other one leaving because they will both know that while breakups are always sad, they can take care of themselves when they're on their own. The more inner work we do to release baggage and be good to ourselves, the more we will attract people who have also done a lot of growing and self-work. If we get healthy, we will attract healthier people. Imagine that.

How to Fill Yourself Up

- **Become** the person you want your mate to be. For example, if you want someone to take you on elaborate road trips, start planning road trips with your friends. This will fill your wanderlust.

- **Love** those around you exactly as they are and don't try to "help" them improve by giving them advice. By being more accepting of people, you'll attract someone who allows you your own process and to be as you are. And by the way, unsolicited advice giving is just bossy, not helpful, and it generally causes resentment.

- **Give** more to yourself. Instead of feeling like you need to get love, you can give love. Pamper yourself, give yourself enough sleep, buy yourself a gift of appreciation, take yourself for massages when you need them.

> *The best remedy for those who are afraid, lonely, or unhappy is to go outside, somewhere where they can be quiet, alone with the heavens, nature and God. Because only then does one feel that all is as it should be and that God wishes to see people happy, amidst the simple beauty of nature.*
> *—Anne Frank*

How to Get Over Your Neediness

When we feel we need love, we come off to other people as "needy," which causes them to feel the very thing we fear: they feel repelled. Then we start holding on tight to everything we have, which is exactly why we don't get filled up. Contrary to what it may seem, the way to feel filled up with love is to give love, not horde it. If you often feel empty this is a clue that you may want to focus on giving more love to those around you.

For example, Janice was feeling needy and unloved one night, and she wanted her partner to cuddle her and make her feel happier. Though he does love her and cuddles her often, on this particular night he just turned over and went to sleep. Janice was furious. She felt that he wasn't loving and didn't care about her.

> *Men and women, in general, have somewhat different needs. A woman needs to feel heard and tended to in a relationship. Ideally, she needs to be noticed, wanted and adored. She needs to feel treasured by her feelings. She needs someone who will anticipate her wishes and take action to fulfill them, even before she thinks to ask. She needs her partner to keep his word to her. She needs him to be someone she can count on, someone who will do his best to make her feel secure.*
>
> *Men on the other hand, need to feel needed. A man will thrive when he feels appreciated by his partner and when he is acknowledged for his accomplishments. Too often, women remember to acknowledge a man for his big accomplishments but forget the little things that he does each day to make her happy. He needs to be acknowledged for these little things, too. He needs to be accepted just the way he is. He will thrive if he feels admired, authentically liked, and respected. A loving partner who encourages and inspires him will bring out the best in him.*
> —Katherine Woodward Thomas, *Calling in "The One"*

What was really happening was that on some level he sensed her neediness that night and it felt like someone wanted to get something from him—as if Janice was a vampire that wanted to suck life out of him. He thought it would be exhausting to make her feel happier that night, so he turned over to ignore her and pretended not to notice her neediness.

Janice on the other hand was outraged. She felt he was not meeting her needs—a job that she thought he signed up for. Janice was coming from a place inside, from way back when she was a little girl and her love and attention needs were not being met.

What Janice could have done differently that night would have been to nourish herself by reminding herself how much love she actually had in her life. Love never disappears; it is always there. We decide if we want to tap into it or not. She could have done this by thinking about all the good things she had: a loving family, a nice apartment, friends she adored, incredible success with Marni. She could have realized how grateful she was that she had this man in her life. They had fun together, they both enjoyed watching hockey, they were extremely sexually compatible, they had similar tastes, they made each other laugh.

> *All you need is love, love, love is all you need.*
> —*John Lennon*

As Janice filled herself up with her own thoughts, she could then have turned over and expressed how much love she felt for him right then. Instead of trying to get love from him, she could have given it to him. In feeding him love, she would also have been filling herself up and creating her own happiness, which is far more empowering than trying to get what she needed from her mate.

Relationships Bring Out the "Stuff" We Need to Heal

It seems like when we're single we want a relationship, and once we get into a relationship the grass on the single side of life seems so much greener. We think about how much easier and less convoluted our life

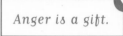

Anger is a gift.

was before he waltzed in. Suddenly it seems as if he is the source of a lot more stress than he's worth. He's driving us mad and making us wonder why we ever wasted our lipstick on him.

The truth is that love brings our *stuff* to the surface. These feelings have always been there, waiting for a catalyst to bring them out. Relationships are those perfect catalysts. Part of the purpose of relationships is to learn and grow. We can't learn and grow without bringing out the old stuff to be looked at, learned from, accepted, and discarded. We cannot absolve our old monsters without facing them. If we don't acknowledge them, they will come back to haunt us with the next person we date. This is one of the sucky things about being a part of the human condition.

Know that anger you may feel toward him is not really about him. It is usually about something deeper. Even if he was an asshole that cheated on you and dumped you, your anger is still ultimately about some other time, earlier, when you were treated badly or abandoned. There is a saying: "If it is hysterical, then it must be historical." Meaning if you're seething and hysterical, it is most likely rooted in some other, older wound. Sit with your feelings and see where they come from and then console that old part of yourself that needs the love. Be grateful that this man, even if it feels like he's not worth shaving your legs for, is bringing out old wounds to be healed.

As One Finger Points Forward, Three Point Back

When you point your finger at someone saying, "You did this and this and this," chances are those are your issues being brought up to work through. If you're attracting unhealthy guys, see where you're unhealthy. This sucks because we don't always want to see our own shadow. We would much rather focus on his. Let's face it, having a real connected relationship takes so much energy. It can be scary and bring up tons of internal stuff that has been just waiting to burst through. Self-work is challenging work but the benefits are amazing and life long. Living on the surface of a relation- ship does not allow for a deep connection with your lover.

Saying Sorry

The beauty of apologizing is that we are able to accept our own faults and forgive ourselves as we ask for forgiveness. Instead of being adamant about not apologizing—"But he should be apologizing. He is the one that picked the fight in the first place!"—we can instead find acceptance within ourselves for our own stubbornness. We can forgive ourselves for being only human and allow an apology to be as much an offering to ourselves as to him.

Forgiving Even If We Don't Want To

Forgiveness is necessary to letting go and moving on up. A lot of times the resentments that we hold on to from past relationships—with lovers, with parents, with siblings—are precisely what have blocked us from getting into new and better relationships. So how do you forgive when you still feel pissed, but you know you have to let go of the anger in order to move forward? Forgiveness can feel so damn hard at times.

The good news is that while we think the feelings of sadness or anger have to be worked out before we can forgive, this is not always the case. You don't necessarily have to *feel* like forgiving to forgive. Forgiveness can be something that you decide to do and focus on just as you would any other goal. When you focus on giving energy to the intention to forgive, the hard place inside that doesn't feel ready to forgive will inevitably begin to soften. Your willingness to forgive is actually something that you have absolute control over.

Day 28 Exercise: Confront Your Anger

Recall an event in which you found yourself seething with anger. Okay, even if you weren't *seething*, ask yourself if the anger was misdirected. Consider the following questions:

- Did I feel threatened? Why?
- Why was I so annoyed?
- What was I scared of?
- Why did I feel compelled to blame?
- Why did I feel hurt?
- How did my reaction align with my emotional patterns?
- What did I fear losing?
- Did I have expectations in this situation?
- What does this pain remind me of?
- When did I first feel it?

The answers to these questions will help you confront anger, stop blaming, and speed up your growth.

Day 29: Breakups and Moving On Up

What is a date, really, but a job interview that lasts all night? The only difference between a date and a job interview is that in not many job interviews is there a chance you'll end up naked at the end of it.
—Jerry Seinfeld

Dating brings up all our hopes and fears: mend me, fix me, don't leave me alone, save me, be my financial savior, make my life fun and exciting, marry me and take me away from this lonely life. If we were already well aware of these parts of ourselves and how to comfort and relieve them, we would have much more fun dating, and the fear of rejection wouldn't be so big. We would know we are enough as is. If we dropped our expectations of someone filling up our emptiness and focused instead on simply having fun, we wouldn't suffer because we wouldn't have expected so much. We could look at dating as a way to learn more about ourselves, to have fun, and to develop more compassion for others.

Our aim in dating is to try to show our authentic selves so that everyone knows what they are getting and there are no surprises. And, if we've done our own work on removing baggage and making ourselves happy, showing off our authentic selves can be quite delightful. Who wouldn't want to show off their genuine amazement at how interestingly their lives are unfolding? We only try to be what someone else wants us to be when we don't think we are good enough. We become afraid we will lose that person

Dating brings out the best and worst in us, so bravo to you, you brave soul.

if we let them see the real thing. When we know we are enough as is, we are okay with letting down our guard because we know it's going to be okay. We can take care of and love ourselves, and we don't need anyone else to do that. It would be nice if they stuck around, but we understand that we are a delicious carrot cake and a lover is really delicious icing. So when we discover that his chocolate icing won't go with our carrot cake, it's okay to end it. We're both great, we're just not a match.

When a Date Turns Sour

You are totally and completely allowed to make a run for it if you are miserable. Robyn went on a date with this guy to explore a museum, have dinner, and go to a movie. She knew at the museum that she didn't want to continue with the date but she went to dinner and the movie and then went back to his house. They ended up fooling around and eventually got it on. *What?!*

This is your life and your time. Your primary job in life is not to make *him* feel good. Your job is to make *you* feel good. We're not telling you to crush him, but don't waste his time, nor your own. Sure, we don't want to hurt his feelings. We don't want to be mean and reject anyone. But

> ### When Does It Sink In?
>
> *It takes men about six weeks longer than women for big, emotional discussions to sink in. So if you break up with him and wonder why he isn't sobbing like you, it is because it hasn't sunk in for him yet. Give it time. Don't call, and about six weeks later, when you are just getting over it, he will start feeling down. Women are more emotional so we go right into our feelings, whereas men go right into denial and avoidance.*

remember, if you'd rather be at home reading a book, the act of going home to read is more valuable than hanging out with this cowboy. Women can be too nice and too worried about hurting someone's feelings and not busy enough taking care of themselves.

How to Quickly Get Out of a Bad First Date

If you are on a first date, try and make it so you can scram quickly. Always have enough cash on hand to pay for a cab or drive yourself. It's harder to end it early if he's your ride home. Since we're on the subject, you shouldn't get into a car with a guy on a first date anyway. We would love to assume people are safe but have you seen the movie *Monster?*

Here are a few strategies for getting out early:

- **Lie about a bad headache.** The old standby works. You can say it once, let ten minutes pass, say it again, let ten minutes pass again and say, "You know what, I might just have to go home. I'm not feeling well, and I don't know why. I think I had some bad hummus earlier today." He'll look at you and think, who would make that up about hummus?

- **Kindly tell the truth.** It's okay to say, "I don't think I want to be on a date right now. It's not you. I'm a bit panicked/tired/distracted/.... I need to take care of myself and go home. I'm sorry if your night is screwed up. This is what I need right now." If he's not a guy that can handle that, it's good to know right off the bat. He may think you're rude. Whatev.

- **Cut your losses and say you want to go home.** Marni actually said once, "I'm in the middle of Harry Potter, and I can't stop thinking about what's next." The guy thought she was weird and was happy to send her home.

Breaking Up Bravely

When all sucks and you just want out, we think you should give him the dignity of proper closure—even if you'd rather just never call him again. If you cut him loose in a way that feels good to you, you won't have to worry about bumping into him, avoiding that coffee shop you occasionally see him at, and so forth, because you'll know your side of the street is clean.

Being brave counts for something. It's a hefty deposit into the karma bank. Let the breakup be an opportunity for you to grow by facing a fear. And don't feel guilty about wanting to break it off. You're experimenting. You are supposed to be testing different waters. It doesn't mean something is wrong with him or something is wrong with you; you two just didn't click. As we said before, his chocolate icing doesn't go with your carrot cake. You're in the market for cream cheese icing. No biggie.

When you bravely break it off, you're saying yes to what you really want. You're telling the entire Universe that you want more. Not only are you being polite, dignified, and gracious in the way you treat him, but saying no to something not right for you will bring you closer to the person who is right for you. Plus, you're sending him closer to the person that is right for him, which means you're practically a saint for dumping him. And, it puts an end to old patterns of unclean breakups. Breaking up the right way may feel difficult at first but you will get better at it. Plus, when you have a clean breakup, he might be more apt to set you up with his cute friend.

Ten Highly Effective and Kind Ways to Breakup with a Guy

Instead of breaking up with him the same way, especially if you've broken up with him multiple times (hey, it happens), try to switch up the reasons why sometimes. Here are some examples:

> *You've got to get over this, Marni. It's like you're obsessed.*
> —Marni's dad, Bernie

1. **Just friends.** "I've had so much fun with you but I don't like you in that way. I would love to just be friends." Most guys will take this as a hint not to call. Although you said you wanted to be friends (even if you're secretly not interested in being friends), they will take this cue. If he calls you anyway, call him back *only if* you feel like it and only when it is convenient for you. If he doesn't take the hint and is still calling because he still thinks he has a chance, or is calling under the guise of "friends" and you seriously don't want to be friends, you are under no obligation to call him back.

2. **Move on.** "I've had so much fun with you but I think it's time for me to move on." It's good to keep the focus on yourself. "I really want you to know it's not about you because I've really enjoyed spending time with you, but I think this is about as far as we go."

3. **Not ready.** "I've had so much fun with you but I'm not ready to be in a relationship. I want to date a lot of guys." How on earth can he argue? He may also want to date a lot of girls.

4. **Too busy.** "I've had so much fun with you but I have too much on my plate. I'm too busy to have a boyfriend right now." You can add a list of things that make you busy ". . . what with my important work project, the play I'm rehearsing, my photo class, my French lessons, the business I'm starting up, blah blah blah." Buh-bye.

5. **Marriage material.** "I've had so much fun with you but I think we have too many differences, and I don't think you're the one I'm going to marry." This is especially good for the commitment phobic man. "I'm really interested in finding the person I want to marry and have lots and lots of babies with. I *love* babies. This has been really fun though." See ya.

6. **The religion card.** "I've had so much fun with you but we don't share the same religion and that's important to me for a long-term relationship." Even if this isn't

Always start with a compliment when breaking up with someone.

really the case, he can't argue with you. And if he wants to convert, continue with "and I really want to be with someone who shares the same culture as me." This is also known as the culture card. If he shares your religion and culture, refer to reason 4 above. You're just too damn busy. What is a girl to do?

7. **The ex card.** "I've had so much fun with you but I've decided to get back together with my ex." You can also say you're not over your ex and aren't ready for something new. No one can compete with history. "But I've liked spending time with you, and you deserve to find a girl that is right for you." See ya, wouldn't want to be (with) ya.

8. **Not sure.** "I've had so much fun with you but I'm not sure I'm ready to date right now." It's okay to be uncertain but it's not okay to ignore him and pretend dating him never happened. Maybe this breakup is still leaving room to possibly date him again. You're just not sure and that's okay.

9. **Bad timing.** "I've had so much fun with you but I'm still getting over my last relation-ship." A rebound relationship is okay if you let him know that is what this is. When you're getting over another relationship you may feel empty and want to be filled up.

This new guy may be filling you up but once you're full you may want something better. Chocolate icing ≠ cream-cheese icing.

10. Maybe next month. "I've had so much fun with you but I feel like I really need to be focusing on other stuff right now, not on dating. You seem like a really interesting person and I like you, but right now I feel overwhelmed by other stuff. I probably won't be able to do anything for a month or two, but feel free to call me in the future." This excuse will let him know that you were genuinely interested, but honestly want to focus on other stuff. Then you can decide if you want to go out with him again in a few months. Even if he never calls you after that, you didn't burn any bridges and needn't feel guilty.

It is so tempting to just leave him hanging rather than being up front. When you leave him hanging you get to feel nice because you never had to *see* his feelings hurt. But it is usually best not to leave yourself open to interpretation and then subject him to further rejection. Being strung along sucks more than someone just being honest and kind. Respect him enough and yourself enough not to string him along.

Day 29 Exercise: Questions to ask Yourself after a Breakup

Even if you haven't gone through a recent breakup, this is a good exercise to help you learn from past relationships. Relationships don't end simply because "He was an idiot." Look deeper. It takes two people to have a relationship. The point of all relationships is to learn from them. Don't feel like a failure and like it was a waste of time. Change your perspective. See it as "Okay, now I know he is not the one. I can take what I've learned from this relationship, grow as a human being, and take that learning and growth into the next relationship." Find value. It wasn't a waste.

Relationships are mirrors. If you are allowing someone to treat you badly or not live up to your expectations, ask yourself:

- What is this relationship trying to show me about myself?
- What am I afraid of losing if I let go of this relationship?
- What am I holding on to by staying with him?
- What would need to happen for me to feel better?

Day 30: Our Two Greatest Pieces of Dating Advice

Love. Go ahead and take a gamble. So what if you lose your shirt?
Love's a crapshoot—you don't always hit seven on the first roll.
Keep in mind that a good gamble doesn't sweat every hand.
Remember, not every affair ends up at the Elvis Chapel, but that
doesn't mean that it wasn't worth the trip to Vegas.
—Cynthia Rowley and Ilene Rosenzweig, Swell

You made it! Congratulations. We are honored to have traveled this road with you. Before you set off, we just have two final pieces of dating advice:

1. **Don't go out with someone you don't like**. Sounds simple and logical, right? Well, it took us a long time to learn that one. We can't tell you how many guys we have gone   on second and third dates with who we

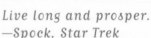

Live long and prosper.
—Spock, Star Trek

knew we weren't into within the first two minutes. We can't tell you how many *relationships* we have gotten into where we knew we weren't into him but we thought that since he liked us we were supposed to try and make it work. Stay open, right? We would keep trying to make it work, keep trying to convince ourselves that we could fall in love with him when we knew in our gut he wasn't for us the first time we met him. Though no date is a waste, once we knew it wasn't a match yet still held on, we wasted his time, we wasted ours, and on top of that we made ourselves loathe dating by pushing ourselves to go out with people we didn't have any fun with. We reasoned that since he liked us, he might be a soul mate and we just didn't know it. Moral is: Go out with people you like. You'll sparkle more.

2. **Be your own best mate . . .** and you'll attract someone just as great as you are. In the meantime, concentrate on making yourself happy and trust that someone amazing will come along and want in on your brilliance. Be your true self, concentrate on making yourself happy, and you'll attract someone truly fabulous. It's magical.

I don't want to make money.
I just want to be wonderful.
—Marilyn Monroe

Day 30 Exercise: Fill Out Your Graduation Form

Congratulations!

You've completed the The Dating Repair Kit course. You now have all the skills required to have a great love life.

_____

(insert your name)

May you go out into the world knowing you are wonderful and irreplacable and have the ability to have a great love life all on your own. You are beautiful.

Marni Kamins

Janice MacLeod

About the Authors

Marni and Janice grew up on different sides of the continent, Malibu, California, and Toronto, Canada, respectively. They came together in their mid-twenties through serendipitous events to embark on a joint career of book writing, teaching, and spreading magic. Their witty banter and beautiful smiles have won them slots on many TV and radio shows nationwide. Over popsicles and chocolate they write books about healing in a fun, wise, and accessible way. Marni and Janice are also the authors of *The Breakup Repair Kit* (Conari, 2004), which has been translated into many languages and is available worldwide. You can reach them at *www.27candylane.com*